EXPLORING CAREERS IN FILMMAKING

By

Robert N. Manning

ROSEN PUBLISHING GROUP, INC.

New York

ANNUAL

MMAKERS EXPO

The call-for-entries by John Fraker for the 10th Annual Independent Film Makers Exposition.

Published in 1985 by The Rosen Publishing Group, Inc.
29 East 21st Street, New York City, New York 10010

First Edition
Copyright 1985 by Robert N. Manning

Library of Congress Cataloging in Publication Data

Manning, Robert N.
  Exploring careers in filmmaking.

  Bibliography: p.
  1. Moving-pictures—Vocational guidance. I. Title.
PN1995.9.P75M33 1985   791.43'023   85-10757
ISBN 0-8239-0641-8

Manufactured in the United States of America

About the Author

Nick Manning lives and works in New York City in film and video production. He holds a PhD in Visual and Performing Arts from Syracuse University and has spent the past twenty-five years both teaching and making films and tapes through his small company, Green Mt. Cine Works. His productions range from a reverent series of documentaries on the people and customs of his native Vermont to feature-length television specials such as *The Other Side of Nashville*, which analyzes the country-music establishment.

Manning has taught at several colleges, both film and video production, and for twenty years has directed one of the largest and most influential festivals of short film and video in the country: the New York Film/Video Exposition.

Most of 1978 Manning spent in India under a Fulbright grant, teaching at the Film and Television Institute of India and traveling throughout the subcontinent making films for the national television system.

Manning has served on the juries of many film festivals and competitions, including the Emmys, the Academy Awards, and the Oberhausen Kurtzfilmtage in West Germany. He is as enthusiastic about the profession of film and video today as he was in 1960 when he handed in his first roll of film to a laboratory.

Contents

Introduction   ix

I.   *Skills in Filmmaking*   1

II.   *Documentaries*   35

III.   *Marketing*   58

IV.   *Industrial/Educational Films*   70

V.   *Commercials*   87

VI.   *Film as Business and as Art*   93

VII.   *Teaching Film*   103

Appendix   109

     Film Production Grants

     Film-Related Unions and Guilds

     Recommended Periodicals on Film

     Film Distributors That Handle Short Films

     Film Festivals and Awards

     Film Schools

     Showcases for Independent Film and Video Work

Bibliography   127

Introduction

"Theatres are the stores where customers buy entertainment but, unlike most merchandising outlets, the buyer doesn't take his purchase away. He pays for it and looks at it, then leaves with only a memory of it"

—Samuel Marx

The responsible filmmaker learns to mix creativity with good business practice early in his career. Often it is the "art" that gets one interested in film, but the bottom line is what keeps one in it. The business is fueled by money, and knowing how it is raised, spent, and protected is important. In the preface to *The Movie Business Book*, Jason Squire describes film as a "cyclical industry, difficult to chart, rooted in creativity and intuition, capable of euphoric profits and dismal losses, engaged in an ongoing seduction of the paying audience." Squire goes on to describe filmmaking as "an enormous crapshoot" ... "where an entire investment is made before anyone knows if the product is marketable."

One of the most successful producers in Hollywood is Russ Meyer. His feature *Super Vixens* was made for $219,000 and has recorded box-office sales in excess of $16 million, one of the top 100 of all time.

Meyer's films are called "exploitation" films in the trade. Most films, in a sense, exploit sex, violence, and so on, but Meyer's films play to basic emotions more directly, to put it mildly. Still, they show a sense of humor and wit and a lack of pretense that has earned him the respect of his peers. Of course, I should point out that anyone who makes a financially successful film gets respect in this business. I believe it is useful to cite Russ Meyer, however, because he seems to exemplify the combination of qualities that has always helped to get careers started. Meyer keeps his budgets low and handles as many elements as he can by himself (he was a photographer in the Army during World War II), including promotion and distribution. None of his twenty-three films has lost money, and he remains a model for many "independent" film producers today. In fact, keeping the cost of features down is currently an obsession in Hollywood, and—a bit like the U.S. government trying to reduce its deficit—it is easier said than done. In 1981 forty-five films brought in more than $8 million in domestic rentals. The average cost of producing those films, exclusive of marketing costs, was $11,335,600, and that average rises by 10 percent each year. Most producers and directors are alarmed by these high figures and, like Meyer, are bypassing unions, avoiding big cities, and hiring young hungry production crews and untried actors. This is where you, the reader, come in. As long as you don't mind being exploited a bit yourself, these beginning producer/directors who are forced to bypass the union are the best way to approach the industry. Keep in mind that when people stretch their finances it can lead to rubber checks and long-unpaid overtime, but such "basic training" is something that most professionals go through and look back on as a valuable experience. Don't assume that just because you are willing to work for little or nothing it will be easy to get on a film production set. Having an unreliable or inexperienced person on the set could prove costly, and producers and production managers are cautious of people who come to them without references.

Every filmmaker recalls how he or she got started in the business. In her book *Making Films Your Business*, Mollie Gregory tells of a producer who decided to learn filmmaking in order to document a family safari around the world. He read every book he could get his hands on until he understood how films were made, but then the trip failed to materialize. "Disconsolate, my wife and I decided to go back to finish college. Before we left San Francisco, I drove down to the camera store to take one last look at the beautiful Bolex I had so set my heart upon. It was raining when we returned to the car. We sat in silence for a long, long time. If there are critical moments in a career, this was one for us. Somehow we both knew what it had to be. I walked slowly back unaware of the rain. I bought the camera, the lenses, the meters and tripods and from my worldly fortune of $5,000 for school, I wrote a check for $1,800. Then I started to learn to make films."

All this brings us to the most important single element in getting started in feature films. You need to meet people. Get to know filmmakers working in the area you are interested in, and keep up the contacts you make. Everyone in the business understands what it is like to start out, and most are sympathetic; but, by the same token, most went through a gauntlet of experiences that "matured" them, and they feel you should too.

Chris Campbell, President of Praxis Media in South Norwalk, Connecticut, summarizes the attitude of most young professionals:

> I don't think it's tough to find a job in this business. I think it's tough only if you haven't fully decided that you're going to do it come hell or high water, and if you try to get in by traditional methods. Sending out 8,000 résumés just doesn't work in this industry. Without exaggerating, we get around fifty résumés a week. It's difficult to pay attention to them. A form letter annoys me because it means that the person isn't being very selective and is probably applying virtually everywhere. If I get the impression from the letter that we have been selected as one of ten or twenty companies that this person really thinks they want to work for, then that interests me.

Campbell goes on to say that a beginner should "acquire incredibly good writing skills" and watch every film he can, because "you will get more out of them than you will out of the classroom."

Movies are a group endeavor. Critics are fond of looking to the director as "auteur" or artistic kingpin of a production. It has been my experience that the crucial contributions to a film can come from any or all of a group of six or eight essential technicians: writer, director, cinematographer, editor, production designer, producer, production manager, and actor. As with any group effort, each person needs to know with whom he is working and how to get along with them. Being able to function as a team player may be the single most important factor in establishing a career in film. Start doing what you can do best, but be flexible; it doesn't make sense to be rigid about what you want to do until you have tried it. It is hard to work "partially" in film; either plunge in or leave. But you should look before you leap. That is what this book is all about.

I have approached the film profession by describing the more important roles and the skills and traits it takes to play those roles. I start out with Hollywood, but only because it is the most visible; i.e., you have read so much about it. But the bulk of the information I provide is aimed at the practical task facing you: breaking into the industry. This is never done at the Hollywood feature level at the start of a career, and even if you have "an uncle in the business," you would be lucky to survive without first working in some of the less glamorous areas such as the noncommercial short film and documentary. Of course, less money is involved in these areas, but less pressure also, and it is the route that most take to a job in the industry at any level. I devote a lot of space to nonfeature-length film work from the point of view of an independent film producer, a phase that most producer/directors feel is the best way to understand the entire process of production and marketing.

Perhaps some of the information contained here will help you get a production out to an audience. Showing others your work is the best calling card you can have, and the only way to become "known" by your peers. Never forget that your teachers are rarely a realistic contact with the industry. Contact is achieved by going to the places where films are made and sold (inevitably a city), showing people what you can do, and persevering until a position opens for you. Remember, you have a lot to learn, and experience is the best teacher.

The satisfactions that come with work in film are significant. It is a flexible art form that permits a wide range of artistic expression. For a businessman it is a risky but often very profitable enterprise, with a colorful past rooted in American tradition and culture, and constantly changing, dynamic. It has the power to reach out to millions, linked to a network of television receivers that spans the globe. What we say with this medium, the tales we spin, reaches a larger audience than had by any other medium of communication in history.

The book that you are about to read breaks down the film profession by individual skills such as cameraman and writer. It also categorizes the field by how those skills are employed, such as feature filmmaker and teacher. To give you an idea of how to approach this diverse profession, and the advice that follows, I have prepared a chart that helps to explain what *general* skills are needed in what areas. Aside from the many specific skills employed in making, selling, and teaching about films, four general skills are required:

1. *Conceptual skill*. Films are nothing more than ideas that have been visualized. Coming up with those ideas is the foundation of all creative art, but among all art forms film stands alone in complexity and cost. That means that one's conceptions must be tempered with a knowledge of marketing and with practicality.

2. *Organizational skill*. Because of the matrix of skills and knowledge required in filmmaking, it is necessary to understand how people work together. Hundreds of people work on a feature film. An individual can develop a skill, but that skill must be joined with others for the system to work.

3. *Visual skill*. Understanding how film captures reality, how motion pictures can tell a story, is the fundamental skill for filmmakers. It is essential to know how we see things; it spells the difference between writing a book and making a film.

4. *Production skills*. These are the most obvious skills: the manual dexterity needed by a camera operator, the critical perception of sound quality by an audio technician, an editor's sense of timing, and even a producer's sense of what people will enjoy watching.

To help understand where these skills are best employed in the motion picture business, consult the following chart. If you think you are strong in a certain skill or would like to develop that skill, the chart can give you an idea where you might end up working. Each of the general areas in the chart is described in this book.

---

1. Samuel Marx. *Mayer and Thalberg: The Make Believe Saints*, New York: Random House, 1975.

	Rating	Category
The producer buys the concept, through the script, and hires the technical help to get it to the screen.	☺ ☺	PRODUCING FEATURES
This area is almost totally devoid of the creative aspects of filmmaking. It is a matter of knowing the market for the product and the people involved.	☺	MARKETING FEATURES
Production skills are like the skills of carpentry, photography, or illustration. They are used by filmmakers but often are isolated from the script-to-screen process.	☺ ☺	MAKING FEATURES
Artists are the same in all media. They must understand how their ideas can be translated in the film medium, but they often hire the actual skills of production and marketing.	☺ ☹	ART FILMS
Documentarians must have a strong idea and the technical skills to conceptualize it on film. Aside from fund-raising, few are involved with the selling of their product.	☺ ☹	DOCUMENTARIES/ SHORT FILMS
Industrial films are often farmed out to people with specific skills, and the scripts are often not strong on originality.	☺ ☺	EDUCATIONALS/ INDUSTRIALS
This is the one area in which it is important to understand every aspect of the motion picture-making process. If a teacher hasn't at least tried to shoot, write, sell, and produce, how can he teach?	☺ ☺ ☺ ☹	TEACHING

EXPLORING CAREERS IN
FILMMAKING

Chapter **I**

Skills in Filmmaking

"Be careful what you wish for . . . it might just come true."
Anonymous

Like many other professions involving the arts, filmmaking should be considered only by those who find it fascinating. Most people who choose to make a living doing something they enjoy never regret their decision. The crucial element in a career decision, however, is knowing what the career is *really* like, nine to five, day in and day out. The person who is entranced by the process of shooting film must learn to balance those moments of euphoria as a cameraman with the job of selling the result, or waiting to be hired to shoot someone else's film. Like musicians, filmmakers often discover a great difference between amateur and professional practice. People who look toward film as a career often forget that it is, after all, business in which standards may be compromised and individuality sacrificed to the needs of a client. Because of the enormous cost of making and distributing films, professionals do not enjoy much creative freedom unless they are independently wealthy or have extensive credits to recommend them.

The purpose of this book is to tell you what it is like to make a living at filmmaking, as cinematographer, editor, producer, director, distributor. Unfortunately, few schools teach the harsh realities of the workaday world because few teachers have any firsthand knowledge of that world.

Rarely do you encounter a teacher, even in college, who has ever had to survive on his skills as a filmmaker, or to please a client with a commercial product. Most teacher training treats film as a fine art, covered as you would the field of English, useful for appreciation and personal expression, seldom looked at as a profession.

But we are going to look at film as a profession, by analyzing each specific skill that is involved in the making and marketing of films: how one gets paid for those skills and the kind of life-style one can expect as a professional. You may discover that you have a special knack for set design or animation. You may get a sense of accomplishment from the home movies you have shot or the play you have directed, but before you even dream of plying your newfound skill in the marketplace, read on to learn what lies in store.

Let us first look at the skills of filmmaking from the standpoint of the feature film. A documentary cinematographer has a very different job from that of a cinematographer on a 35mm feature, so it is important to know something about the differences between these types of production.

In the 1940's, when Hollywood was famous for the studio system, people worked together as a team on films, and the result was enviable. Films such as *Citizen Kane* were made with crews that had worked for years in RKO's sound stages with their own props, cameras, lights, and so on. But Hollywood, as anyone who has taken one of the famous studio tours can testify, has largely abandoned its studios to shoot on location. The few remaining studios produce primarily for television and are organized by strong unions.

If you visit a set for any theatrical or "live action" film, you will be struck by the specific roles that everyone has. Most films today are produced with crews that are assembled from a mix of independent workers, are quickly pooled together for a few weeks for the photography and recording, and disappear as quickly as they came—only to pop up again in a slightly different configuration for another production in another place. It sometimes reminds me of a carnival going from town to town, putting tents up and taking them down.

Because each film production is carefully calculated to be shot as quickly as possible, to keep down the cost of rentals and salaries, everyone must know how he fits in, who is in charge, and how his job interlocks with others. The only way to learn these roles is to work on a crew, even if it is necessary to start as a production assistant or in some menial task that gives you the right to hang around the set. In that way you meet people who can recommend you in the future and gain the experience to help you discover whether your personality fits the life-style you observe. Features are usually pulled together by a producer, either working independently or for one of the well-known "majors" such as MGM. Once this producer has chosen the property or subject he wants to film, the first person he turns to is a director, who sees to the scripting and eventually the realization of that script on film.

Director

The director is the person who has artistic command of the "set" or the crew on location. In the U.S. the producer or the people with the money keep the final measure of control, even with relatively well-known directors, but they usually do not interfere on a set. Their differences with the director, usually regarding budget, are ironed out in private. A film director needs to instill confidence on a set. There has to be one unifying vision for a film, and an experienced crew knows enough to rein in the impulse to argue or criticize the director. Since most features are done out of sequence in different locations, it is a hard job to keep track of all of the various parts, to be sure they mesh, and the director is often the only one with a vision of how it will all come together.

It is a difficult job, almost impossible to do without experience. Every once in a while a prodigy like Orson Welles comes along, but most directors work their way up through the ranks. Richard Lester came to feature directing through directing commercials; Haskell Wexler, through cinematography, Martha Coolidge through producing documentaries, and Mike Nichols through acting. These names may not all ring a bell in your memory, but it would be worthwhile to consult your library's periodical indexes for articles that discuss their careers. As you look through these magazines you will come across numerous articles on film directors; don't let that fool you. It is only recently that the press has focused attention on directors such as Alfred Hitchcock and Francis Ford Coppola. For years the director was an unsung hero while actors attracted all the attention.

It is important to note that despite the attention of the press, the entire industry is really very small. By Hollywood's definition, a major studio is one that produces at least fifteen films a year. In 1983 there were only six such studios, and this meager output was over half of the total number of features produced in the U.S. India, a Third World country, produced four times as many films in the same year.

Most of the best-known directors make a small number of features in their lifetime. This elite group of approximately three hundred directors have a lot of time between productions to write treatments and scripts and help the producers pull together the financing. Many directors find long periods between films exasperating. Since most features involve spending over a million dollars, it means a lot of paperwork: approvals, budgeting, contracts, market analysis. In some countries producers are willing to turn financial responsibility over to a known director like Jean Luc Godard or François Truffaut, but ever since the movie moguls of the 1930's such as Selznick, Mayer, and Fox, producers in the U.S. have retained control over money during all stages of production. When all is said and done, Americans treat film like any other business. American producers look at a director as they would a painter they had retained to do their portrait. They assess his work and—instead of saying "Paint my portrait"—they hand over a script and say "Make it into a movie like your last one," or like some other film that was a proven box-office success.

Many scripts in their early stages come to producers through a director. This gives the director more power in his constant struggle for artistic control. A producer knows that a film cannot be made by committee or with constant need for approvals, so there comes a point when the director is cut free, put on his own. That point usually comes when the producer or the financiers of the film have been given a clear idea of what the director will do with the script and have acquired confidence in the director to pull it off.

Having a "track record" of previous films helps enormously in this constant battle. I recently met with Sam Ramie, whose horror film *Evil Dead* was meeting with great success at the box office in New York. Sam wrote his script when he was nineteen, financed it when he was twenty, and shot it at twenty-one. In order to get the money for his low-budget (around $400,000) feature, he appealed to small investors willing to take a high risk by investing in his film. That meant that he had to pledge nearly the entire profits to lure in the investors. I remember talking with Sam under the Broadway marquee of his film as he explained that he did not have enough money to pay for a hotel room in New York City that night. A copy of *Variety* under his arm listed the gross income of his film at over $3 million.

What Sam Ramie did gain from his three years of work was a track record. He proved that he was responsible, understood how to please an audience, and could get skilled filmmakers to work with him to get quality product out quickly.

For those who would like to get a shot at directing before they are middle-aged, it would help to study the methods of people like Sam Ramie, who rolled up his sleeves and set out to make a specific film, literally ignoring the big studios. Another person who took the bull by the horns was Armand Mastroianni. In 1977 Armand was in his twenties, living in Staten Island, New York, with a wife, a child, and a small mortgaged home. He worked for his father, who made jewelry, and on the surface it appeared that he would soon be a full partner in the family business. But Armand was fascinated by the idea of making a film—of making people cry, laugh, and grip their theater seats in horror; so he set out to locate a writer. He found one in Brooklyn, and together they dashed off a script about growing up and trying to break out of a claustrophobic Italian-American community in the shadow of New York. The script was sensitive, humorous, and had a touch of pathos; it was everything Armand's teachers at the College of Staten Island had taught him was "good" film.

After nearly two years of trying to get someone to back the production with Armand as assistant director or in some capacity where he could get a production screen credit, Armand decided to make a short film to go along with the script to demonstrate his ability to direct. He put notices in *Backstage* for actors willing to work for nothing, rounded up a volunteer crew, and made a half-hour drama. The 16mm film was well produced and attracted attention from several producers, who pulled out a script for a low-budget horror film and asked Armand to direct it. He leaped at the chance and produced *He Knows You're Alone*, a perfectly dreadful 35mm feature about a deranged killer. MGM took in over $8 million at the box office for this "first" film within a year of its release.

It isn't unusual that the two people I have chosen to discuss made low-budget "horror films" to start their careers. People as well known as Francis Ford Coppola started with this genre, with its almost guaranteed audience. There seem to be fewer risks when a little blood is splattered about. Despite the fact that this type of "B" movie may disgust you, if you want to make films you would be wise to take any opportunity that comes along to learn film technique. Very few directors start out choosing their material. Feature films are risky enough without taking a chance on an unproven director.

Cinematographer

Most people would agree that the cameraman is close to the director in importance in making features. Some directors take a strong interest in the "look" of the film, and others enjoy concentrating on the actors and leave the camera to the cinematographer, who is almost always referred to as the Director of Photography. My personal preference is for the director who concentrates on getting the actors to make sense of the script and leaves a good cinematographer alone to decide on camera angles, lighting, and so on. Films like *The Black Stallion* emerge from such partnerships.

The last ten years have seen a surge of interest in cinematography in schools. One reason for this is the technical improvement of "raw stock," or the color film used in 35mm and 16mm cameras. Kodak has developed several sensitive color negative films that free a cinematographer from cumbersome lights, permitting real locations and natural lighting. The cameras have evolved in the last twenty years from the cumbersome 35mm Mitchell, which took at least two men to lift, to light and silent cameras that can be hand-held and moved about with stabilizing devices that permit the cameraman to be more creative than ever before. This new portability has attracted more women to the

Cartoon by Theo Pingarelli. A cinematographer sometimes finds it difficult to separate his personal feelings for a situation from the needs to exploit it for all the dramatic potential it contains.

field, but there are still very few women cinematographers in the professional ranks.

Cinematographers find the effort to work up to a serious feature film as difficult as does a director. Since cinematographers are generally looked at as technicians and hired for the duration of the shoot, one person can shoot four or five films a year. That leaves only a few openings for beginners and a long trial period before getting a chance to work.

The typical cinematographer is first a technician. He must understand the mechanics of many professional cameras, the characteristics of film stocks, and how to light a scene quickly. All directors of photography began as assistants, or camera operators, so they know the workings of the camera firsthand. It is important above all to pay attention to detail: tiny hairs in the film gate, or a microphone edging into the image. Nobody but the camera "sees" the scene the way it will appear on the screen, and this gives the cameraman a special status on the set. If a cameraman says a light is not flattering to an actor, or a plant seems out of place, nobody, including the director, is about to argue the point. The cameraman, for that tiny slice of time, is at the pinnacle of the production.

Cameramen travel a lot, and most find it difficult, while building a reputation, to have a normal married life. The erratic schedules, long hours, and exotic locations make it a romantic life-style. The cameraman along with the crew forms a gypsy caravan of people traipsing about the world's airports laden with expensive hardware en route to places they may never have time to really see outside their viewfinders.

Directors, when established, usually join the Directors Guild of America, which helps to give them strength when dealing with producers interested in whittling away their share of profits. Cinematographers are less like management and more like labor, and in the American tradition they have strong unions to back them up. Although people who film documentaries, commercials, and industrials often belong to a union, it is the cameramen in the entertainment industry who have the strongest organizations. Known as I.A.T.S.E., the International Alliance is a mighty force to contend with in Hollywood and mandatory to join if you want to shoot features. The I.A. screens all members with rigid tests, but contrary to rumor it is not closed to newcomers. N.A.B.E.T. is the second union for cameramen and in a way is a rival of I.A. N.A.B.E.T. is younger, covering most people on television crews, and is more flexible in its rules, but it still provides a stiff test for aspiring cameramen. It is often the case that you first get a job and then join N.A.B.E.T. after a grace period.

Camera work is very competitive. The life-style and the ability to reach so many people with one's creativity intrigue young visual artists. Films combine different types of artistic expression: photography, acting, music, design, attracting people who like to experiment and test their skills in different areas. Unfortunately, because of the strict role definition needed on feature films, a person with eclectic tendencies should probably think of short films or video, where cost is less of a factor and there is more room for experimentation.

Cameramen may become involved with lighting and aspects of the set that relate to composition and rendition on film stock, but they rarely go beyond that. The framing of an image is probably the most critical element in all production, and it is not something people want to turn over to a jack-of-all-trades. A good assistant cameraman or camera operator is expected to know how to thread a wide variety of cameras (and if you think that is easy, wait until you run across a Milliken high-speed camera) and operate everything from an Eclair film camera to an Ikigami 79 video camera. A good way to pick up this knowledge is to call up a company and offer a free day's grip work if they will check you out on the camera you need to learn. Another way to get started is to ask around to find out who is a good camera operator. Call that person up and ask if he would like some assistance on a shoot. If you can, try to see the person after hours, perhaps at his home, and sit down with him long enough to explain what you can do and what you would like to learn. From there on it is up to you. A reference from a working professional is extremely valuable.

Aside from the stiff competition one faces as a feature camera operator, assistant or DP, it is necessary to add a note of caution to those who turn their talents to commercial production. Film financing is so erratic and risky that producers who are otherwise prudent and honest people may find themselves overextended. In short, it is sometimes difficult to get paid for your work. Lawyers thrive in the film business; there are very few people who have not been given rubber checks at some point in their film career.

Music Consultant

Music for films, like the current hits in the top ten popular charts, dates very easily. The last thing a director wants is a film that is dated by its music, so consultants are often listened to with attention when it comes time to discuss the score or the "track" of a picture.

Recently a rash of pictures like *Flashdance* have begun to rely very heavily on the music for their appeal, evidently cashing in on the wave of interest in music videos. When such films are designed, a lot of thought is put into the music and a lot of care into the mixing of that music. Some films mix down over 100 separate sound tracks made up of vocals, ambience, and different instruments to get a good four- or six-track final print. The sound of a feature film gives it a clear edge over television, where most people listen through one three-inch speaker. Film music is a good field for someone with an ear for contemporary style. The music can be recorded live, it can be scored and recorded separately, or it can be purchased from a library.

Recording music live is rarely done; if it is, the job falls to a sound technician, who usually needs to resort to a mixer to blend the music properly. Writing a score can be another matter altogether. The music must back up the photography without calling attention to itself. One of the most difficult aspects is getting the music to fit the picture, neither longer nor shorter than the scene it accompanies. This kind of compromise most musicians and composers resent, but the fact is that in nine out of ten cases the photography comes first.

Original composition is common only on large-budget pictures. Recorded music usually proves less expensive and avoids the difficulties involved in getting a good recording of original music. Once you have located a piece of music for use in a film, it is necessary to get the rights to the composition and the performance. This can prove more difficult than it sounds. Say, for example, you would like to have some traditional background music. Even a song like "Wildwood Flower," a traditional ballad, has an owner who might decide to sue if there were enough to gain from a victory in court. To avoid all this, one needs to go to one of the recorded music libraries (Valentino and Chappell are prominent in the field) and purchase the music needed. Most of the libraries have relatively colorless music, intended to blend into the background and not draw attention to itself; but they do have a wide variety of moods, and the rights are all clear. All you need do is pay them by the "needle drop," almost like buying bologna by the pound. Filmmakers slice off as much as they can afford for their productions.

Libraries are used extensively by low-budget films and documentaries. To work effectively with these collections, it is the skills of an editor and a librarian combined that prove effective. The music track for any film is like a patchwork quilt. It takes the abilities of a musician, but one who is capable of fragmenting music and weaving it through images and plot to create a mood. Most composers complain of very limited time to work, and almost everyone working in music complains of low budgets. Approximately 10 percent of an average film budget is spent on music.

Sound Recordist

Less visible on the set and rarely thought of by the press as an important figure, the sound recordist is essential for all drama today.

Years ago it was popular for film actors to do their scenes without recording them. The lines would be "dubbed in" later in a special studio and then mixed with other effects or music. This gave the production crew an easier job, since cumbersome booms for microphones weren't needed and everything didn't have to be "quiet on the set." But as mikes got smaller, and even wireless, shooting live sound and picture simultaneously became easier and the realism caught on. Few pictures today are dubbed; sometimes an actor rereads a line or two, but films are recorded on location, and this has put the person who records the actor's lines in a prominent role.

Most recordists own their own Nagra audio tape recorders and microphones, operating like a director of photography going from shoot to shoot. Because of the development of Dolby sound for theaters and the need to provide an experience that a moviegoer can't get at home watching television, sound technicians are more and more in demand. It is a versatile skill also, since video producers also need good sound and the principles are the same.

Recordists are truly technicians, more so than other members of the crew with creative aspects to their role. While cameramen rarely modify or repair their equipment, an audio person is constantly rewiring and patching. It is a field for one who is patient and meticulous, independent, and more a craftsman than an artist.

The job of sound recording can be lonely and downright uncomfortable at times. Here Rolf Pardula is at work on location.

The life of a sound recordist can be very much like that of a cameraman, involving a lot of travel. The principal difference is that a sound recordist does not have the pressure that a cameraman does, so it is easier to enjoy the travel—although there is a lot of waiting around, stuck on the set, while scenes are being set up.

A sound crew is usually composed of two persons, with a third if the budget allows. The principal sound technician operates the mixer, which routes the various microphones through filters and equalizers onto the tape recorder. This person has the final say on what goes on the track. An assistant operates the "fishpole," which gets the mike in close on location shoots, or the "boom" if the shot is in the studio.

A sound person must know the particular qualities of at least a dozen types of microphones and how to place them in a scene so that the pickup is uniform. Obviously, a lot of patching and soldering has to be done to keep things up to par. It is important that the sound person be able to work with the camera operator, staying out of the shot with the mikes, and in documentaries being able to keep up with and almost anticipate where the action will lead the camera.

Sound has leapt into prominence lately. Francis Ford Coppola's *The Conversation* pioneered the use of Dolby stereo, as well as giving the viewer a good idea of the life and personal characteristics of a sound recordist. Television broadcasts will soon be standardized in stereo, and videocassettes (soon to be a major means of distributing films) are touting their hi-fi sound. People, and producers as well, are beginning to realize that one's response to a film has a lot to do with the sound quality.

On feature films sound is recorded on location, but it is often used only as a guide for the dubbing that is done in controlled circumstances in a specially designed studio. These lines, sound effects, music, and so on, are mixed on an elaborate board with a profusion of sliding levers and knobs. Each track is filtered and equalized and blended with the others, some of which had already been mixed on location. The music director may have had to conceive this matrix of sound, but the mixer has to sew it all together, usually with a director and a producer looking over his shoulder and the clock ticking away at $300 per hour.

Sound systems like these are far more elaborate than anything in videotape. Although video programs use a mixer, it is only during the actual recording. Any postproduction recording is usually done only to patch up mistakes. There is far more attention to detail in films, and the mixing studios are better equipped. I was once at the National Film Board of Canada watching a friend's film go through a mix when a scene came up that included several ducks flying through the background. The mixer picked up an intercom and described the ducks, the number, the speed of their flight, and the distance from the camera. In what seemed like less than three minutes the duck sound came through the system. Everyone nodded approval and the film was backed up and started again, this time with the precise sound of the ducks in the background; no one could ever tell that it had never been recorded.

Editor

It is often said that the best directors are editors because they can see how the pieces of the puzzle that make up a movie go together. I'm certain that a director who has been an editor is a more effective and efficient director.

An editor takes the scenes that have been shot and pieces them together along the outline of the script to make a cohesive whole. If all directors were like Alfred Hitchcock, who was famous for a meticulous shooting script, the editing process would be a simple mechanical job. When the typical film has been shot and the time comes to make it "work," it bears only a faint resemblance to the original screenplay. A lot of intriguing scenes just don't work out, actors change, it rains for the longest stretch in recorded history—these kinds of things crop up and put the editor in center stage. The director keeps track of the changes, but it isn't until the editor sits down with the synched rushes that the rhythm and structure of the production take shape.

Editing is an often underrated skill. Most documentaries are shot in such a way that they capture the realism of the moment. Making real life dramatic is hard, particularly when it is necessary to build a story with a rhythm and pacing in keeping with the subject. A good editor is meticulous, patient, and knows how to tell a story. A feature editor has a crew of people to synchronize the "dailies" so that the picture and sound are together, but there is still a lot of "hands-on" work for an editor. A Steenbeck editing machine, which is to an editor what an Arriflex is to a cameraman, is relatively easy to master, but the tedious pace of the work burns out a lot of people after a few years.

Film editing is much more physical than video editing. Video tape editors push buttons and let the tape recorders search the tapes for the cuts they want, building the program from beginning to end. A film editor strips off a take by hand, hangs it on a trim bin, gauges the duration of a shot by the length of the film, building the program outward from key scenes, and then trimming the first cut down to size. Many people feel that this flexibility and direct contact make film a better medium for editing. Nevertheless the trend is toward more video editing, for the simple reason that it is cheaper and faster.

Editing is the one area of production in which women have always been active, and in recent years they have begun to dominate. Carol Littleton is a good example of a successful editor. She earned a degree in French literature and spent several years in Paris doing research on seventeenth-century French literature; then she returned to the U.S. and began to learn editing. Her latest credits include *Body Heat* and *E.T.* She feels strongly that her liberal arts background and her travel abroad helped her in her career. She found the French film critics sophisticated

An editor spends long lonely hours over machines like this Moviola flatbed editor.

and erudite, and many of the filmmakers more politically committed than in the U.S. Her study of literature has helped her sense of storytelling. She says, "The story has to work, and if it doesn't, you have to understand why."

I mention Carol Littleton not because I believe you should travel and study in France to learn editing. Editing can be learned quickly on your own or in one of a hundred schools around the United States. It is the understanding of what it is that you are editing that is important. What is the theme? What is the value of the message? How do we learn from others to improve and enrich our work? If you sit down and talk with outstanding directors and editors you will find them to be interested in ideas and to have studied the past. They have traveled. They read as well as spend long hours watching films. In short, they are curious people. The great directors and editors— and I lump them together because their skills and talents are so similar—are storytellers who draw from an understanding of the past to help us understand life in the present. In short, they are artists who understand our culture and society. Carol's career was helped because she stepped out of her American culture to study abroad. She was able to understand it better because of that distancing. It is my feeling that too few Americans take time from their careers for this kind of travel and study.

A lot of the praise and sometimes even the criticism directed at the camerawork of a film is really the work of the editor. Fast-paced shooting is really fast-paced editing. Editors must be able to work in the claustrophobic atmosphere of a darkened room for months on end.

Aside from the ability to tell a story, editors have to know how to select the appropriate "take" (and there may be dozens to choose from) so that the film flows. But above all, an editor must be organized. Half of the work is filing, storing, and logging roll after roll of film and then assembling that collection in sequence. Some people simply can't handle this kind of detailed, repetitive job, which obviously takes a degree of manual dexterity and an eye for detail that some feel you need to be born with.

Editor-related Jobs. Once a film is finally cut, it is handed over to a "conformer," who goes back to the original footage (an editor works only with a copy, called a workprint), pulls the shots that match the workprint, and splices them together so that the cuts are invisible. This requires splitting the film into two rolls, an "A" and a "B" roll. This is a tedious task that is purely mechanical. No creative decisions are made at this point, but also there is no room for error. A negative cutter, or conformer, is paid by the splice. A ten-minute film has about fifty edits, and the average price is $2.00 per edit. A lot of conformers attach themselves to a particular laboratory, which funnels work to them. Several editors in New York have begun to offer filmmakers a service that includes editing, conforming, and working with the laboratory to assure that the correct colors for each scene are obtained.

It stretches the point, but people who work in film developing and printing are working in the film field. Unfortunately, not much of the glamour or the romance of the art form rubs off, aside from an occasional brush with a director or producer who wants to discuss a technical point. The size of the laboratory work force is shrinking, partly because of automation and because fewer prints of feature films are being made as television grows as a means of distribution. Movielab, once the largest film-processing laboratory in the country, closed its doors in 1984. Many other smaller labs are diversifying, getting into video duplication and transferring from film to video tape. All labs are unionized, and most are full of nepotism, but lab work is one area that a young person, without a lot of experience, can use to help launch a career. "Expediters" function as a liaison between the lab and the production staff of a film. This can be a vital and important position on a film, and the expediter often is recognized in the credits.

How a film is processed and printed can have an enormous effect on its impact on the audience. Processing is not a simple job. The film can be "pushed," causing it to become grainy and more sensitive to light, like the effect obtained in *Elvira Madigan*. The film can also be "flashed," or exposed to light in such a way that the scene appears diffuse and flat, like the scene from *The Graduate* in which Dustin Hoffman is floating in the pool. Scenes can be tinted or filtered in the lab for a particular look. Daylight scenes can be turned into nighttime scenes. Films that involve special effects require special attention by the lab. I once shot an experimental film in the Northwest and needed some special effects for a scene. I went to a small lab, Alpha-Cine, and asked them to try for a particular effect through something called additive printing. The result was a stunning scene that I expanded into a major portion of the film. To this day I do not know the full name of the person who created that effect; all I know is that the work was signed "Claudine."

Writer

Much has been said about the poor, forgotten writer, laboring away in a garret far from the light of the real world, unrecognized and rarely given credit for his work. While we can discount some of this portrait as exaggerated self-pity, there is more than a bit of truth in it. Given their enormous contribution, screenwriters rarely receive much coverage in the press. Few people can name even one screenwriter, yet they can rattle off the names of hundreds of actors and dozens of directors.

Of course, there are others—cameramen, for instance—who are also ignored by the press, but I think we feel a little more sympathy for the writer's anonymity because of the drudgery associated with the work. After the writer has slaved over a hot typewriter (read word processor, in a few years), the script is snatched away by a director and all of a sudden it becomes his; he rearranges scenes and dialogue to fit his mental image of the characters and storyline. By the time the actors add their interpretation, many a writer can barely recognize his original script. It is hard to fault individuals for this professional plagiarism; it is just the way the system works—sometimes for better, sometimes for worse. It is hard to get around the collaborative nature of filmmaking. Sifting an idea through so many different hands sometimes clarifies a point; unfortunately, it almost always destroys a personal viewpoint and threatens the cohesiveness of a storyline.

The most controversial script in feature filmmaking is Herman Mankiewicz's *Citizen Kane*. Both the original script and the shooting script are reproduced in a book by Pauline Kael, *The Citizen Kane Book*, which also includes an essay entitled *Raising Kane*. In this essay Kael accuses the director of the film,

Orson Welles, of stealing the limelight from Mankiewicz by adding his own name to the credits for the screenplay (the only Academy Award the film received). The story of Mankiewicz's life make this little theft poignant. He was a brilliant writer with a drinking problem, at the end of his career. He was vulnerable to a young (twenty-six), ambitious director like Welles, who may very well have extorted the credit from him. But I believe Kael has overlooked a common attitude: Most directors think of themselves as writers. Many enjoy working with dialogue and structure just like a writer, but lack that special constitution that permits a writer to work alone for months polishing and perfecting the often minute bits of dialogue that give the script life.

Writers rarely take up their trade with the idea of becoming rich. People who calculate the odds and plan for a career usually become doctors or lawyers. Like other artists, writers seem motivated by the satisfaction gained from the process of creative expression alone. Although they often go unnoticed in an industry full of hype and hoopla, deep down they know that without them Hollywood would be out of business. Robert Redford has spent several years raising support for the Sundance Institute, which he has established on a Utah ranch. The sole purpose of this "institute" is to help promising young scriptwriters develop and sell their stories. So far, half a dozen films have been made with scripts developed there, and many more are on the way. Many critics of the films of the late 1970's felt that Hollywood was going stale. The term "genre" kept popping up. Although the term is used by film scholars in a legitimate sense, basically it means, "We've run out of ideas, so we're going to do another movie like..." We can be thankful to Robert Redford for his efforts to turn fresh talent toward scriptwriting.

In a talk with Walter Shenson, the producer of *Help* and *Hard Day's Night*, he acknowledged the serious lack of good scriptwriting today but felt that some changes were beginning to show. Shenson felt that the screenplay for *Reuben, Reuben* by Peter De Vries was extraordinary, and as producer of the film he saw to it that the script was followed exactly as written.

William Goldman, author of *Butch Cassidy and the Sundance Kid*, feels that young authors are often deceived in schools. They are never told, according to Goldman, that it is "near impossible to get a novel published today, and if it does get published it might take in one or two thousand dollars. Film writing, on the other hand, can pay very well." Aside from the two hundred or so scripts that are made into films each year, many more are optioned (paid varying amounts for the rights to the script) and even more are paid for through development deals and shelved for possible future use.

If you are interested in writing, put together the best script that you can and send it to agents and producers, whoever you think might either use it or become a valuable contact. This is called a "show script" in the trade, and it may never be produced, but it will demonstrate your talent and it could possibly lead to a job "developing" other scripts on commission. These development deals are popular in Hollywood with directors and producers who have a general idea of what they want but lack the patience and discipline that it takes to slowly build a script.

Writers should be aware that their work on screenplays is vulnerable to changes that can make their ideas unrecognizable. A writer is the initial contributor in a chain of collaborators that eventually results in a movie. Filmmaking is a delicate mix of skills, and it is difficult to do an autopsy on the process to determine responsibility, because it all depends on the interaction of individuals. As a writer becomes better known, he becomes a more important part of the process. Neil Simon is going to be taken seriously by any film director, and William Goldman is listened to by producer and director alike; however, it took these writers a long time to reach that position. Most beginning writers are forced to sell their work with no strings attached and can only cross their fingers and hope that their original intention will emerge in the final product.

In a rare look at the inside of a Hollywood "deal," *Esquire* magazine published (August 1983) a revealing story of the negotiations between director George Roy Hill (*The Sting* and *Butch Cassidy...*) and writer John Gregory Dunne. In a somewhat resigned but bitter tone, Dunne puts the whole process in an absurd light: Hill approached him and his wife, Joan Didion, to do a screenplay for *The Little Drummer Girl*, a John LeCarre novel. After a careful five-day reading of the novel, Dunne set up a meeting with Hill. They set aside a few days to go over the book. Hill came to Dunne's house, and they settled in to work on what the book was about, what the "line" of the movie might be, what might be eliminated, what was necessary. After nearly two days' work they had blocked out the first forty-five minutes of the film. They seemed to be working well together.

Hill asked when the final draft could be done, and they settled on a date. Then Hill went to the producers to talk money and bring the relationship to contract. Dunne settled in for a period of negotiations. He says, "The reason that negotiations take so long in Hollywood—it is common for contracts not to be signed until long after a picture is in release—is that the negotiation establishes the channel of power, the chain of command. Making an individual break down over money in the negotiation process is one quick and clear way to establish that power, to show who is boss. The production company can do this because it has one unassailable advantage: Everyone wants to make a movie. The line is long, the chosen are few, and the chosen learn to suck wind—or someone else is chosen."

Dunne and his wife consulted an attorney, who felt that they should ask for $500,000 guaranteed. He based his thinking on the cost estimate of $20 million for the production, with the producer and director in all likelihood sharing $2.5 million between them.

If you are taken aback by these figures, Dunne's advice is to remember that "the one purpose of the huge fees in the movie business is to establish respect: in the hagiography of Hollywood, a million dollar director has half a million dollars more respect than a $500,000 director." Another adage is that once you have established a fee, your next deal can't be less, and everyone else knows what everyone else is making. In short, Hill offered $450,000, only $50,000 away from agreement, a relatively "small" sum (which shows how far removed the movie business is from the real world). But nothing happened. It was a standoff and the deal fell apart. Neither Dunne nor Hill would budge, and Hill signed another writer, Loring Mandel. I would venture to say that this failure to come to agreement is rare, but the incident illustrates the nature and the scope of the deal-making in Hollywood.

One common fear among writers is that the ideas they put in

their scripts will be used and their scripts discarded. Unfortunately, this is not paranoia. It does happen. A friend of mine had an idea for a TV series lifted from a script and expanded upon by a director who did not credit or compensate him. He took the director to court and won (after a two-year battle), but his career was over in Hollywood. The old adage, "You'll never work in this town again" has a ring of truth to it when you decide to cry foul on a script. The writer is just too vulnerable to defend himself.

One help in this regard is the Writers Guild, and it is the first place to go when you finish a script. If someone does steal your work, you need to have proof that it was done by you and when it was completed. The Writers Guild registers your script and, in effect, copyrights the contents. Directors and producers are always looking for new ideas and read, or have others advise them on, hundreds of scripts each year. A professor from Yale recently sent in a script to the producer of "Hill Street Blues." It was a first effort and unsolicited, but it was read and eventually produced. That particular episode went on to win an Emmy for the show, and the professor is now a full-time writer with an income six times what he was earning as a teacher.

Although a feature script might earn the writer $200,000, only a small number are produced. Television, on the other hand, can't get enough material and it is what keeps most screenwriters solvent. We may sneer at the formulas and repetition in television programs, but the medium has made millionaires out of writers like Joanna Lee, who gave us "Gilligan's Island."

To get started in a production job you can always apprentice yourself by convincing someone of your burning desire to sweep floors, or you can go and make a film and try to convince people that the skills demonstrated in that reel permit you to bypass the preliminaries. With scriptwriting there is only one way to approach the profession: Write a script. Even if you study with the best professors available, it comes down to your ability to write a script that you can send to producers and directors and "pitch" or verbally present to potential purchasers.

Malvin Wald, who after three hundred screen and television credits still thinks of himself as a "struggling" writer, made a survey of fifty professional screenwriters to determine their attitudes and advice to beginners in the Hollywood marketplace.[2] Some of the responses he received are worth repeating here.

Karol Ann Hoeffner (active writer of TV movies): "Major in radio-television-film and be prepared to spend at least a year supporting yourself."

Donald M. Leonard (screenwriter who began in production): "Remember that producers *need* ideas to survive. Go into a producer's office knowing that you have what the buyer needs. They're not doing you a favor—you are supplying blood for the vampire's thirst for survival."

Richard Baer (writer of sit-coms and TV movies): "Be sure that your scripts are in proper form in terms of margins, tabs, line spacing, etc., and remember that neatness counts."

Norman and Harriet Belkin (TV comedy and drama writers): "Just as important as a powerhouse agent is making your own contacts, which can prove to be more important than talent."

John Gilligan (writer of documentaries) on agents: "Don't count on an agent for anything except a 10% deduction from your paycheck. Even so, sign with the best you can. It makes people think you are a writer and not a typist."

Elias Davis (one of the writers for "All in the Family"): "The dividing line between those who make it and those who don't is in the area of tenacity rather than talent."

Art Director

The realism that has swept the screen of late has taken our minds off set design. Period-piece spectaculars and musicals have been put aside while we revel in the realism of New York in *The French Connection* or San Francisco in *Bullitt*. But the art director hasn't disappeared. Aside from "taste," an art director is expected to have an understanding of what the camera lens does to perspective, how colors combine to render an effect that works on film, how textures are created to fool the eye, and how workable inexpensive materials can be used to fake reality.

Every film has a "set" of some kind, and even actual locations need to be improved upon for the right effect. It is the art direc-

---

[2]*Journal of Film and Video*, Vol. 36, No. 3, Summer 1984.

tor's job to see that the set is interesting and in keeping with the film. The skills of a carpenter are useful, but that is a specialized field. Most professionals come through programs in technical theater in college drama departments. Art schools such as Pratt Institute in Brooklyn and the California Institute of the Arts also produce good art directors. Most of them will tell you that school was only a beginning for them. This is a specific skill that one learns on the job.

Actor

Acting is a profession that has been repeatedly discussed in the press and on television. Everyone knows that it is very difficult to enter on a full-time basis, yet I have been involved with casting minor roles in obscure films without offering any payment and seen 250 actors show up to try out.

The great majority of actors have jobs outside of the theater because they know full well how risky it is to find work. This lack of work is partly due to the nature of film and television. In countries like Denmark and Sweden, live theater is popular and actors can rely on enough work to keep them occupied if they are capable. But it takes a lot more actors to put on a stage play than it does to produce a film. Twenty actors working for six weeks can produce a feature film that reaches an audience that numbers in the millions. The live theater is also popular in the U.S., but most actors yearn for at least a try at screen acting. The reasons should be obvious: recognition, an audience a hundredfold more than one can expect in a theater, and for some a shot at that elusive position in the modern world known as stardom. When faced with that kind of payoff, it isn't surprising that so many give it a shot. Television has helped to give many actors work, and there is even a union for extras that helps support several thousand people, mainly in New York and Hollywood.

I have found that a rational explanation of the odds facing young actors is not enough. The best way to understand the problem, and why people refuse to accept the odds, is to attend one of the famous "cattle calls" at which aspiring actors (or perhaps I should say, actors seeking employment) crowd in to try to convince a casting director of their special qualities. Check with the local SAG or Actors Equity office to get information about these calls. *Backstage* and *Variety* also are sources of information on tryouts.

Even if you are convinced that you have what it takes to be an actor, plan to spend several years trying out for parts, doing bit parts for nothing or next to it, and taking lessons from teachers with the latest technique. To make it through this kind of trial period, you need a profession. Too many ignore this and end up waiting on tables or washing dishes. Kate Capshaw, the female lead in *Indiana Jones and The Temple of Doom*, was a teacher for years right up to the time she was cast for the film. Most actors have another profession with which to support themselves, and they mark their final acceptance in the acting profession as the time when they could afford to leave it behind.

If you are able to go into a job search with the attitude that you are playing a lottery with long odds, it could certainly help to have some academic training to back you up. There are, of course, many good drama schools in the U.S. and England. The University of Washington and Yale University are particularly distinguished schools with a traditional broadly based program, but many film actors have found that a special school such as The American Academy of Dramatic Arts works best.

You can improve the odds a bit if you can begin to narrow your goal. The odds for steady work, if you aren't hooked on Hollywood, are better in New York. Five thousand people in New York make a living acting in commercials alone. Add to those brief stints a job or two on the road with a trade show or an industrial film and once in a while a spot on a soap opera, and before you know it you are making a respectable living. This income isn't short-lived either. Because of union minimum scale regulations and the concept of residuals, checks for one spot selling soap can come in for months or even years.

In this business everything is at the last minute. You'll need an answering service to catch those late casting calls, and you'll probably find that living in or near Manhattan is necessary. It is an irony of the business that a person will come to New York from rural Minnesota to work as an actor only to be cast in a commercial aimed at a rural Minnesota audience. Why don't they cast right in Minnesota? I can't answer that question, except to say that New York is where one goes to find professionals. It is where the agencies are and the casting is convenient, and it contains the largest pool of actors of all types in the country.

Keep in mind that not all acting need be like performing on stage. For example, for anyone with a good voice there are opportunities for "voice-over" work. Some "actors" help make ends meet by modeling one attractive feature, such as their hands, for commercials and are paid well for their time. I recall one man who simply held a product in his hands for a close-up and was paid $500 for his two hours of "work." I doubt that many people would contemplate launching a career based on their photogenic hands, but the income can help one get through the low points that crop up in every career.

The agent is a must if your career catches on, and if you can find one willing to take a chance he can help you get that start. Most jobs are farmed out to agents, and even casting calls are funneled through agents, who see to it that their clients get the first shot at whatever jobs come along. Woody Allen's *Broadway Danny Rose* chronicles the life of an agent, and despite the obvious humor injected into the film, it comes close to the mark in describing an agent's role in the business. The agent's standard fee is 10 percent.

It is not necessary to be exceptionally handsome to get acting work, but you need to fit a particular type: "ethnic" (Italian, Spanish, etc.), "all-American," "Yuppie." In commercials the chances of your getting work will depend more on the current popularity of your type than on talent or looks. Of course a popular type and a dynamite agent only lead up to that final step that you take all alone: the audition. How you come across personally will make the difference. You will need a résumé with a picture, which your agent will help you develop, but in the final analysis it is your talent, or personality, or look that will pull you through that last hurdle.

The only advice I would venture to give in handling a call or an audition is to try to understand the sort of character they are looking for. If it means coming dressed for the part, then go for it. You may be thinking Shakespeare, but if it is Bozo the clown they want, learn to make a fool of yourself.

Acting is the one area in filmmaking where unions reign supreme. Once you land a job, and can get your employers to admit that you aren't taking a part that another union actor could do (pro-forma if they really want you), you will have to join the Screen Actors Guild or the American Federation of Radio and Television Artists. It is a simple matter of signing a form, but the union ranks are swollen and approval might be denied if you can't show that you have had serious professional interest such as college training or summer stock.

Miscellaneous Positions

A film on location is like an army on the march. It needs cooks, drivers, communication specialists, and a host of other people that one doesn't think of as being part of the film profession. These jobs may lack glamor, but they represent a very good way to get a look at or even a start in the business of making films.

Locations Specialist. Every film that is not shot in a studio must find a "location" in which to shoot. This can be a long and difficult task, particularly if the film is to be shot in, say...Orlando, and the central character lives in a Victorian house. Somebody has to go out and find that house, talk to the owner, and negotiate an arrangement to use it. The necessary electrical power has to be located and brought to the house; bathroom facilities for the fifty to one hundred people who end up working on the set have to be rented and brought there; maps must be made up to help people find the place, caterers scheduled, police permits obtained, and so on.

Most of the work that is done on location is handled by the production manager, but his work is made much easier if someone finds a place that has enough power, space, and parking. A locations specialist is a valuable person to any production, and the job is a good way to help get a career in producing started. I have known two producers who began their careers finding locations for feature films.

Production Manager. Because the production manager is so vital to the everyday needs of cast and crew alike, he reigns on location. He is second only to the director in importance when things get active. A PM sees that the crew calls (when the various crew members are needed) are posted, the cast is scheduled for the right scenes at the right time, and everyone is paid on time.

Shooting time is short because of the high cost of labor and equipment rental, and a set can be chaotic. Everyone is there to work hard; they bring their skills and their tools and punch in. If the PM doesn't make their assignments clear and free from conflict, the production can run over, and that can spell disaster. If the set is mostly union workers, they will demand overtime or, as it is known in the networks, "golden time," which doubles and after a while triples their wages.

Production managers must understand every element of the production. A PM runs a kind of command post where all information on the logistics of a production is coordinated. It is a strange position in the sense that a PM is like a midwife, helping to birth production after production without much input into the creative aspects of what is being produced.

Special Effects. An EFX specialist is a combination of makeup artist, sculptor, and chemist who uses latex, explosives, dyes, and a collection of mechanical devices to give pizzazz to a film. The exploding cars in James Bond films are the work of an EFX team. Horror films like *The Evil Dead* use imitation blood, plastic skeletons, and smoke machines to enhance the drama of the show. EFX teams design breakaway sets for films like *Squirm* in which millions of worms crawl across the screen and miniature sets for films like the *Star Wars* series.

This is obviously a highly technical field. It may be more like the job of a professional magician than of a filmmaker. Find a master at the trade and apprentice with him; that is the only way to pick up this business. You can experiment with explosives (after obtaining a pyrotechnics license) and learn to operate a fog machine on your own, but mixing latex for *The Blob* or rigging a mechanical wolf for *Wolfen* requires experienced guidance. Lee Howard, one of the best-known special effects artists, has a laboratory like an alchemist's shop in a fairy tale, filled

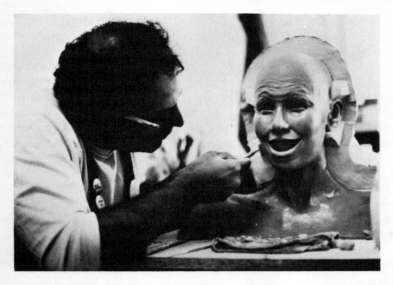

Special effects or EFX have become an important part of the movie business. Here Ken Meyers works on a prop for Silent Madness.

with all manner of chemicals and plastics. The trick is in knowing how to use these compounds to replicate reality; in short, to work magic.

Grip and Gaffer. One difficulty for the beginner is that these positions are unionized. The grip puts up sets and adjusts lights, pushes dollies, and so on. Gaffers are essentially electricians; they determine, with the director of photography, where the lights will be positioned. Getting this kind of experience is not easy. Work as an electrician would certainly help, since a film set can easily use over 50,000 watts of power, which is dangerous to use if you are not experienced in three-phase 220 power.

Both of these positions are physical. A lot of hauling cable, setting lights, and laying track is involved, so much, in fact, that these men often don't know much about what is being shot.

Makeup and Costume Design. If you are the kind of person who sits through the credits at the end of a film, you know that at a point the names begin to roll faster up the screen. Those last names zipping by, readable only by the people named and their relatives, represent a lot of vital and unrecognized talent.

A makeup artist works very long hours, always arriving before the cast and almost never absent from the production. Since a lot of films extend their days to ten to twelve hours of working time, the tedium of waiting between the scenes can be a problem. Dealing with makeup is highly specialized and obviously a skill that is developed through practice. Aside from the normal makeup that every actor wears, there are the more challenging jobs of aging people, giving Marlon Brando a new look for *The Godfather*, or making Roddy McDowall look like an ape. It is not pure artists' vanity that creates work for makeup artists. Cameras respond to color and skin tone differently than does the naked eye, and a little embellishment is called for in even the lowest-budget film. The book *The Technique of Film and Television Make-up*, by Vincent Kehoe, helps to outline what it takes to make it.

The costume designer also has a challenging job, but very different. Where a makeup artist is out in the front lines, rubbing elbows with the glitterati, the Cinderella of the set is busy shortening or lengthening garments or selecting wardrobes. A costume designer, also covered by a union, starts off as a dresser, working closely behind the scenes with the actors. The next step is to supervisor and finally to the quaint title of "first person," supervising all the costumes on the production. This term, like many others, is part of the jargon of the trade.

Script Supervisor. The title "script girl" has recently been modified, in the light of the new sensitivity to sexism, to script supervisor, but the meaning remains the same: keeping track of the film from scene to scene so that the scenes, when edited, will match. This may seem like a menial job, but because films are always shot out of sequence, it is easy for an actor to walk out of one scene wearing a red tie and into the next with a green one. A script supervisor keeps track of these things and makes sure all the scenes in the script are actually shot and will fit together in the edit.

Free-lance

We have discussed various positions without much consideration as to how one gets paid. You can work for a production as part of a permanent staff, such as you might find in an audiovisual production unit in a college or corporation; or you could work for a short time on a specific project. That is free-lancing, and it is the way most people get work in today's market. The golden days of RKO with a permanent staff are long gone. On most low-budget productions, everyone but the producer and director is free-lance.

A free-lancer often has a specialty, such as operating a steadicam or shooting under water, to help him or her to stand out from the pack. But no matter what job is done, the life-style of the typical free-lancer is what makes or breaks the position for most people. For some reason the peripatetic life-style, the travel, and the absence of a boss looking over one's shoulder seems to appeal to people with talent in film production. Independence is important to most people who work in the business, and I dare say most would fight against a return to the regular paycheck on a staff somewhere.

Coordinating from one job to the next is the single most difficult problem facing a free-lancer. One can sit around for months and then get three rush calls for work on the same day. Because the work is sporadic and to an extent seasonal (winter is slow), it is difficult to refuse. Many free-lancers find themselves without vacations because they are afraid to turn down a job. The call might never come again. That leaves a person chained to work, unable to let go and develop any kind of home or family life.

To make a success of whatever skill or talent you employ in this business, you will need to be able to get along with people. A crew is a closely knit group from two to twenty people who have to function amicably for the duration of the production, which can be up to ten weeks for the average film. Finally, as in any endeavor, one needs to be able to show up on time, build and maintain a list of contacts, and establish a backlog of experience that proves reliability.

Middleman

We have methodically gone through the traditional positions people occupy in filmmaking, but I don't want to give the impression that the business can be broken down so easily into neat compartments. A great many people contribute a great deal by simply expediting, coordinating, making deals, and getting key people together.

As you begin to develop an understanding of the skills and see the process of filmmaking more clearly, you realize that the real money, and the risk also, belongs to producers. Some of these producers are lawyers or businessmen who have analyzed the possibility of making a buck and who move in to work in film in the same way that they would buy a tanker of oil for resale. These people aren't blinded by any desire to produce art or to move people, except to stand in line for a ticket. This calculating capitalist approach often clashes with the "labor" whose talent is committed to making the project work. For those people who have lent their talent to film, it is difficult to move up in the ranks to producing. A good producer must distance himself from the film in order to make objective business decisions. William Randolph Hearst made picture after picture with Marion Davies as a star. The films were total failures. He was blind to the fact that she was unsuited for the stiff formal roles in which he saw her.

Hollywood is filled with middlemen, with one foot in the art of film and the other in the business. It sometimes seems that everyone is trying to put together a deal of one kind or another. There is a note of pathos in these potential deals because of the difficult odds. But just when you think they are pipe dreams, another *Melvin and Howard* story comes true. Deal-making, I have decided, is really a valuable talent in the filmmaking process. Knowing how to mesh the financial needs of backers with the creative talents of filmmakers is a skill that often goes unnoticed.

I had occasion to visit a friend in Brooklyn recently. He had fallen from his motorcycle and injured his back, so the visit was partly to cheer his convalescence, but I also had an ulterior motive: I was curious how his career was coming and thought a chat with him might be worth including here.

Aleks Rosenberg, closing in on forty, is an animator and special effects artist with many industrial and commercial credits to his name. He has also produced several music videos. He was alone as I arrived at his newly decorated apartment. Alex had gone in with a partner and bought a three-story building in an out-of-the-way area of Brooklyn. His apartment, more like a loft, was stark white and filled with his paintings and sculpture. We sat down at a desk near a window looking out on an industrial landscape, with the taller buildings of Manhattan just visible in the distance.

RM: How is your work coming these days?

AR: I haven't really worked on a serious project for several months. I've been trying to put together a deal to put music videos on cable stations, and it has taken forever to send letters to all the people involved. I don't have any idea whether the deal will go through or not, and at this point I'm beginning not to care.

RM: You're not doing any animation these days?

AR: A relative of mine came to visit New York a few weeks ago, and he asked me what I did for a living. You know, I had a tough time trying to explain to him just what I do. The fact is that I don't really do anything specific, like shoot or direct, and I am really not interested. I can find people to shoot my animation. I can find plenty of talented people to do just about anything I want. I have just lost interest in doing those things. The most important thing is to pull together a project. If I get tied up with the details I am wasting my experience. There are plenty of people out there waiting for work. Somebody has got to pull these details together so that we can all get to work.

RM: Have you tried bidding on contracts lately?

AR: The problem with contract work is that the people who are letting out that work all have relatives or friends that they see to first. If a project comes along that demands a specific skill that you and you alone have, then there isn't any question; but otherwise it is a very tight fraternity with interlocking favors. It is hard to break into that circle.

RM: And the music videos?

AR: Forget them. There are so many people who want to get a start by doing those that you have to pretty much do them for cost to get a contract. I'm just not interested any more.

RM: What kind of project are you looking for?

AR: I need to pull together this cable packaging deal to get some stability in my finances, but I would really like to do a feature. A good story with a good budget is what I'm after. I'm looking for scripts to option, and I haven't run across many good scripts out there. I'm almost tempted to sit down and write one myself. Everything I see today is teenage wish fulfillment, a kind of visual bubble gum. I'd like to see some serious stories or comedy like *The Gods Must Be Crazy*, which I thought was very funny.

RM: Any advice for beginners?

AR: It is easy to think of filmmaking as director, sound technician, etc. But there comes a time when you realize that producing is the primary job. Not too many people make it as straight labor in this business. I started out as an animator, and look at me now. I think most people move around in this business, and very few end up where they thought they would be at forty. So, I guess, versatility and being able to capitalize on opportunity are the key traits that help.

Chapter 11

Documentaries

"Some artists turn from documentary to fiction because they feel it lets them get closer to truth. Some, it would appear, turn to documentary because it can make a deception more plausible."

Erik Barnouw

A documentary is a film that provides information, usually through observation or interviews with people who are not actors.

A lot has been written about the film documentary. To understand the range of films that fall into the category, Erik Barnouw's history, *Documentary*, is a classic text.

During the 1960's a revolution took place in filmmaking. The equipment, usually under the control of studios and unions, began to become available at prices the average person could afford. This was because of the extensive use of 16mm cameras for television. As television grew, it relied upon 16mm technology for news, and the equipment makers began to mass-produce inexpensive cameras and recorders. Schools began to teach filmmaking, and the use of film for artistic expression expanded like a genie let out of a bottle. One form this expression took was the documentary; it was put to use to rectify the social ills of the sixties and to usher in a new era. The limited funds of individuals were soon supplemented by federal granting agencies, and social documentaries sprang to life.

A documentary is a film that provides information, usually through observation or interviews with people who are not actors.

Social Documentaries

The documentary film gives a powerful voice to a person who feels there is a wrong in society to be made right, an oversight or a problem we will face in the future. "60 Minutes" is consistently one of the highest-rated programs on American television, but it is a very small voice in a chorus of filmmakers who have decided to examine various social issues. There is no country in the world that even comes close to the prolific production of independent documentaries in the U.S. Unfortunately, unlike CBS, these producers do not have a convenient way to get the documentary seen by the public. Several festivals, such as the Film-maker's Exposition in New York, provide a forum, but it really remains up to schools, libraries, and television stations to locate and show these documentaries. Our public television stations appear to be more interested in "safe" and popular programming than in showing challenging documentaries. One of the few programs in New York City that regularly programmed short, independently made documentaries was Channel 13's "51st State." It was canceled after running for several years and never replaced.

All this leads to the conclusion that if you are interested in making a documentary film you are likely to: (1) have trouble finding people to pay for it, and (2) discover that once finished you need to work even harder to get it shown.

Raising money for short noncommercial films of any kind can take far more work and time than actually making the film. Applying for a grant can easily take a year, and often you discover that after all the paperwork is done the stimulus to do the film has disappeared. Probably the best example of perseverance went into *Harlan County*. Barbara Kopple spent years patching together small grants to make this $250,000 documentary on coal miners that went on to win an Academy Award. After that prize and national acclaim, her film was blown up from the original 16mm to 35mm and distributed nationally; a few days after its release it was playing to empty houses. People expect social documentaries on television, but they certainly don't want to pay for them. *Harlan County* will never recoup its original cost. The film's director benefited by being associated with a winner and got an inside track on funding for new projects; but if any of the funding for her film were "at risk" it would have been lost. When a film like this runs into financial problems, it should be a message to all documentary filmmakers: Don't do it unless you can afford to lose the capital you put into it, and the cost of the average broadcast-quality documentary today is close to $1,500 per minute of screen time.

Despite the obstacles, making a documentary film can be enormously influential and personally satisfying. To get the film distributed, filmmakers initially depend on television. This is the largest total audience for documentaries, but it is a general, undefined audience suitable for some ideas, but not for others. The slower method that can eventually amount to the largest audience is sale to libraries with film collections. Once the film is reviewed in magazines that cater to librarians, such as *Library Journal*, preview films or tape copies are sent and sold to those that like the film. Despite a headlong rush to move production to video, these libraries still prefer film. It can be seen on a large screen, and they have the reliable, simple equipment with which to project the image.

Nick Manning filming a program on child labor in Pune, India.

Another source of revenue lies in the large audiences in Europe and Asia. Many new documentaries are recouping their costs in Europe before even opening in the U.S. *The Other Side of Nashville,* a recent two-hour documentary on country music, will probably make more money in Europe and Japan than in the U.S. because the rights to performance are less expensive there, and easier to obtain.

If you are able to handle the financial problems either through raising money by persuasion or obtaining a grant, you have licked the major obstacle to making a social documentary. Making the film is technically complicated but easy to do because there is an abundance of well-trained filmmakers usually willing to pitch in (for reasonable compensation) out of sheer love of the process. The most serious mistake one can make is to entrust a film to people "committed" to the idea of the film. The crew needs to be capable of quality camera work, sound, editing, and so on. If they also believe in the premise of the film, fine, but first and foremost they must understand the nature of the medium and be skillful in working with it.

Despite the attention the press accords the makers of documentaries on social change, only a few hundred are active in the U.S., and they produce fewer than fifty films of any consequence in a given year. The bulk of documentary production is by television stations.

Television Documentaries

Television stations are mandated to produce programs of value to the community in order to remain licensed by the Federal Communications Commission. A few of these programs are still shot in film, but most are quickly cranked out with video equipment, saving the station's time and money. It is theoretically possible for these programs to be of high quality, aesthetically pleasing, and insightful. But, for a variety of reasons that I will discuss later, video simply doesn't deliver. After serving for seven years as a juror of documentaries for the National Academy of Television Arts and Sciences (which awards the Emmys), I can safely say that the best work is done on film. I have found also that the best video documentaries are shot by people with a film background, leading me to the conclusion that even if you plan to make a career in television documentaries, it pays to learn by making films. The process is slower and

During the late sixties filmmaking became associated with social and political problems as a way to get the message out to the world. Here a student in a film workshop for minority teenagers in Detroit turns his Bolex on the world.

easier to control, giving the beginning motion picture producer-/director more time to experiment and attend to details that could be crucial in establishing a reputation.

No matter what the medium, tape or film, the nontechnical elements remain the same. A person who likes to meet and get to know all kinds of people makes a good documentary filmmaker. Personality means a great deal. People have to feel that they are being treated fairly and that the people recording their thoughts and feelings care for them as people and will respect their individuality.

A typical documentarian is a person interested in social or political problems who finds the power of the media useful to reach people with new ideas or to raise their consciousness. Such a person can easily be frustrated when working for television stations, which have one objective, to make money. The managers of TV stations try to spend as little time as possible on obligations like documentaries unless they can draw some attention through a scandal or exposé. Even the prestigious "60 Minutes" has been accused of sensationalism and exaggeration of the facts regarding General Westmoreland's role in assessing the size of the enemy in the Vietnam War. Television documentaries are done generally by young people who are learning the ropes and who move on up in the establishment, passing the job on to another person after a few programs. As a form of journalism, the documentary is enormously powerful, but within the commercial confines of the American television system a true journalist often finds it too restricting. Some issues simply can't be elaborated in sixty minutes, or pass the scrutiny of sponsors. "The Guns of August," a documentary on the sport of hunting, was literally killed by the CBS sponsors, who did not like the critical tone of the piece. Some people find the problems of raising money to do documentaries on their own less difficult than putting up with the restrictions of the broadcast industry.

One reason the bulk of American documentaries produced by television stations are not of high quality is the modus operandi of the stations. Usually a TV personality is chosen to narrate (can anyone ever forget Ted Baxter?), news crews are assigned various interviews, and an editor pulls it all together with the "director" looking over his shoulder. Even the director can lose track of these scattered elements, and the results show on the screen. The only independent documentarians working with a network are Jon Alpert and Keiko Tsuno, working for the "Today Show." PBS recently formed a consortium of five stations to produce "Frontline." This weekly series of hour-long documentaries appears to be the format that offers the most hope for the future of televised journalism.

Anthropological Documentaries

The scientific filmmaker deserves some attention in the field of documentary production. Many of the people working in this field are experts in science or social science and pick up skills in filmmaking to assist them in their research. Film is essential in time and motion studies. One can freeze motion that is too fast for the naked eye and compress long events like the growth of a plant into a short span.

But these useful aspects of film are specific skills that are appended to other professions. The field of anthropological documentation places film at the center of the research. Notable films like *The Hunters* and *Dead Birds* recorded African tribes going about daily routines in a way that let the audience slowly draw their own conclusions about the way of life of these people. If the social documentary is trying to persuade with a distinct point of view, it can be put at one end of a spectrum. At the other end is the anthropological documentary, which rarely persuades but subtly informs by recording events. Many people, not only scientists, have begun to realize the value of film in understanding human behavior. The Challenge for Change program run through the National Film Board of Canada has used film to help people address their problems. They have dealt with questions such as how Indians can retain their cultural roots in a modern industrialized society, or how people can learn different trades when their old means of making a living disappears.

To make this kind of film takes a special kind of person. It often takes months, even years, to get the needed footage, and the living conditions can put a strain on the strongest constitution. Film has not been challenged by video technology in this field. Harsh climates wreak havoc with electronic cameras and recorders. The simple mechanism of film cameras makes them reliable and easily repaired. Since much of this kind of coverage is for preservation in archives, film also wins out over tape. The continual change in video formats, from 2-inch, to 1-inch, to 3/4-inch to 1/2-inch, and rumors of an 8mm format in the wings, gives one little confidence that we will be able to play back what we have recorded in the future. It is close to impossible to play tapes recorded twenty years ago. What assurances have we that the quality of our polyester videotape of the 1980's is that much better than the acetate of the sixties? It would be a shame to wait fifty years to find out that it is unstable. At least we know film will keep an image for a minimum of a hundred years.

The universal choice of documentary filmmakers is 16mm film. It is capable of being screened anywhere in the world and broadcast in any country. Television is entangled in a variety of formats (NTSC, PAL, SECAM) and a complex technology that isn't dependable when far from a repair facility with sophisticated diagnostic equipment.

An annual festival of the sort of films we have called "anthropological" is held at the Museum of Natural History in New York. It was named for Margaret Mead, whose work with Gregory Bateson pioneered the use of film in anthropological study. Attending the festival will give one a good look at what to expect in this field.

Crew Positions

The names for various crew positions on a documentary are the same as on a feature, but the actual jobs are quite different. A cameraman on a "verité" documentary, which stresses the natural and unaffected qualities of real people, is in effect the director of the film. The cameraman must decide what to film without consultation with others. The real "direction" comes when it is time to edit, to select what to keep and what to throw out.

In a "talking head" documentary, popular with television stations, the cameraman is relegated to the job of composing the shot and making sure it is recorded. Everything is shot on a tripod, mostly interviews, with lighting the only creative element. A "verité" cameraman may have to carry a camera about for days waiting for spontaneous moments to occur. The sound recordist is in a similar position. Doing typical television work, the most challenging task may be finding a place to pin a microphone, whereas on a more naturalistic shoot one might be dashing about with a directional microphone or wireless trying to keep up with the subject and still stay out of the shot.

In short, the documentary film, and in particular the kind that tries to catch a slice of life, can be a serious challenge for the crew, whereas the director is often relegated to raising money and looking at the results.

Grants

Feature films are made by people who want to make money entertaining people. The documentary film is usually funded by grants, by scientific or cultural organizations, or by independent filmmakers who wish to speculate.

The principal federal agencies that fund documentaries are the National Endowment for the Arts (NEA) and the National Endowment for the Humanities (NEH). Anyone can apply to these agencies, as long as it is done through a nonprofit corporation that will keep the books on how the money is spent. The American Film Institute permits you to bypass that restriction and apply as an individual, but the competition is tough and the amounts of the individual grants are restricted. Most states have programs to fund film projects. New York, for example, provides CAPS (creative artists and producers) grants in addition to support from the State Council on the Arts. Vermont, California, Washington, and several Appalachian states have discovered that supporting the arts can be good business and a way to publicize the unique character of the area.

So, the money is there; now you have to figure out how to get it. The trick is in writing a persuasive proposal. One agency, delegated to fund proposals dealing with social problems with NEH money, recently announced that it had read 423 proposals and funded 12 of them. Those are the kinds of odds an applicant faces. It should be obvious that to get started by this route you need to be able to write clearly and persuasively. Because the best filmmakers are often not that good with words, a small cadre of professional grantsmen has arisen who ask either a fee or a piece of the action.

If you prefer to do it yourself, all it takes is a clear idea of what you want to do. You would be surprised to discover how few people can succinctly explain what they want to accomplish. There are a dozen books on how to write a proposal, but I have found that the best advice comes from the granting agency itself. If you draft a proposal and submit it well in advance, most agencies, and especially the fully staffed endowments, will tell you what is needed to improve it.

Even if you get approval at this stage, you will need a sample of what you are capable of producing. If you don't have anything to submit, I recommend that you find someone who does and go into partnership on the project. This coattail approach is common practice, and even well-known directors will lend you their name for use in a proposal they like. After all, they will be paid if the project gets off the ground, and it isn't any trouble simply to give your project a nod. Arthur Barron, a well-known documentarian, has lent his name to projects with which he had nothing to do until he took a few weeks out to direct.

Assuming you have the right people and a clear, concise proposal, be sure to show how the film will meet the needs of a specific audience. Recently there has been an effort to demonstrate that artistic projects receiving federal funds are seen by people and that the issues are not partisan or political. Do that, and you are almost home.

The final element is the budget. Here you would be wise to seek out a guide. Prices are constantly changing, so it makes no sense to provide actual figures at this point. But keep in mind that it is not wise to try to do a project for less than the current rate. Federal agencies in particular expect to pay full costs so that things are done properly. In 1984 it would be necessary to budget approximately $200 a day for a camera operator, $150 for a sound recordist, and $75 a day for a production assistant. A writer might be expected to receive a flat fee of at least $1,000 for a short noncommercial film script. It wouldn't be out of line for the director to receive $2,000 for a film that could be done in a month or two. Use these figures, which I draw from actual productions, only as a general guide to the level of funding that you can expect to receive. Remember also that the producer usually owns the rights to the film and retains all the profits, except from the perfunctory PBS screening, for the life of the film.

Proposal Writing. Feature film producers spend nine out of every ten days of work on raising money. Even documentary filmmakers spend more time raising money than actually making films. The intricacies of limited partnerships and other methods for getting the capital to make a film are too detailed to go into here. But what is worth discussion is the common denominator in all productions that use others' money: the proposal. A proposal is a three- to five-page presentation usually aimed at prospective investors or granting agencies. No matter who is providing the support, the same questions need to be answered. The only way to avoid writing a proposal is to pay for the production yourself, and even then it is useful to have an outline of what you are doing to help guide those working with you.

Every written proposal should be as clear and succinct as possible. Among the inner circle, Hollywood features are often funded on the basis of verbal presentations, which are in essence the same as a proposal. A good proposal should have the following features, not necessarily in this order:

1. A clear summary of what is to be accomplished and why it is important, valuable, or lucrative.
2. Why it is needed. Are others trying to do the same thing? Is the time right?
3. Who is to make the film, with their qualifications and credits.
4. A realistic budget, including any other support; many federal grants require matching funds to be provided. Salaries should be at or close to prevailing union rates. An organization should be in place to administer the funds and make accountings to the grantor.

Following are some suggestions as to how a proposal can be made more effective:

1. Be sure the people you are working with have qualifications that mesh with the proposal. Don't be afraid to ask experienced people; you may be surprised at how many could use a little extra work.
2. Be sure the project is reasonable and can be done within the time and budget you have allotted.
3. Try to underscore the benefits or usefulness of the project to the community or society at large.
4. Be creative; the key element in all proposals is the originality and freshness of the ideas.

Independents

An independent filmmaker is one who has decided to stand apart from established organizations, to make a film apart from a company that provides a salary. The person can be commercial or noncommercial but is willing in either case to take full responsibility for the outcome of the work. Unlike other businesses in which large volume is the most efficient way to operate, film seems to function best when production groups are small and independent. Film units in large companies or in government are notoriously inefficient. One notable exception to this is the National Film Board of Canada, which produces a remarkable array of good films each year. I can't speak to their cost efficiency, but the results are enviable. Somehow the British tradition in government was carried through in Canada. I am not sure we could manage as well south of the border.

Fortunately the "independence" of grant recipients in the U.S. is preserved in our federal grants, but there has been a trend toward making only matching grants. These provide only half the production costs, leaving the producer to raise the funds for completion elsewhere. Even in the best of times, funding has never been what one could call plentiful. Beginning in the Reagan administration, the endowments and the Corporation for Public Broadcasting began to move toward support of less controversial projects. In 1984 the NEH (which granted $4.4 million to documentary production in 1983) issued guidelines that eliminated projects that "advocate a particular program of social action or change." Surely NEH won't eliminate social documentaries from funding, but filmmakers who see themselves as essayists will begin to dwindle. Already half the effort that goes into a typical film is to raise money. The additional time it takes to find a match from private sources or foreign television may discourage many and take so much time that the issue loses immediacy.

Distribution

No matter how it was funded, your film needs to be screened. The world is unlikely to beat a path to your door. Most filmmakers turn, at this point, to a professional distributor, who takes 30 to 40 percent of the film's income but sees to it that it reaches an audience. At one time distributors paid the filmmaker an advance against profits from the film to help him get back into production and as a sort of pledge of faith in the film. This no longer takes place, but the alternative, distributing it yourself, can wind up as a big headache. Librarians demand preview prints, which invariably end up scratched and torn. It usually takes nine previews for each print sold. A 15-minute film costs about $100 to print and usually sells for around $300. This is a slim profit margin unless a large number of films are sold. Getting the word out can take time, and it is more efficient if films are grouped together and sold through catalogs by distributors. A filmmaker is at a psychological disadvantage at the completion of a film, because the instinctive reaction at that point is to begin thinking about the next project. It apparently is difficult for many filmmakers to turn their work over to a stranger for distribution, which leaves them no other alternative than self-distribution. Every year a few new "distributors" pop up with a film or two. Most of them are independent producers who decided to handle their own work, because a larger distributor felt it would not be popular enough to take on or wanted too large a share of the profits. Only a few of the small distributors last. Even with the larger companies such as Films Inc., the profits have been slim of late. It is not an expanding field.

One of the best ways to get a film seen by potential distributors is to enter it into a film festival. The Appendix gives a list of the best in the United States. Once you've tried those festivals, you could enter your film in a European festival. Berlin, Mannheim and Oberhausen are German festivals that can lead to contacts with German television or other European television systems. Others include Nyon in Switzerland, Edinburgh in Scotland, and cannes and Lille in France.

The American festivals are a much better opportunity for immediate value. They are mostly well run and don't tie up your work for long. These festivals are a great place to see what is being made, get new ideas, and burn out some of the old ideas you may have been harboring. If you enter your own work you should look for these characteristics: (1) a good jury of at least four or five persons; (2) some kind of prize money (a ribbon is fine, but be careful of being used); and (3) a low entry fee. I don't trust organizations that charge noncommercial filmmakers over $25 to enter a festival. I have run the oldest film festival of national scope for nineteen years, the New York Independent Filmmaker's Exposition, which has put over $40,000 in the hands of independent filmmakers and provided detailed criticism from the panel of judges year after year. Try to attend such a festival of short films and get a look at the potential of the film medium. Thinking of film as only features is like looking at a zoo and seeing only elephants.

Television

The best way for an independent filmmaker who has speculated on a production to make money is to go directly to television. A station, or a network if you are lucky, will pay for two screenings during a specific time span like a week or a month, then hand your film back to you to take elsewhere. The amount paid varies greatly. A lot of very small regional stations live on the feed from the network, and if the film you offer the program director points up some local issue, he might buy it. Usually television stations want a series of programs, which are easier to advertise, but exceptions are made. It is rare for a major network to acquire an independently produced film, because of union restrictions. A feature-length drama is the only exception. The best opportunity today for all sorts of film productions lies in the cable television field: Home Box Office, Showtime, USA Cable. This kind of distribution is simple enough for the filmmaker to handle, but several organizations specialize in cable distribution and have a good track record. Coe Associates specializes in films for young people, and Picture Start handles mainly films that would be considered "art." Cable rates are low, but there are a lot of stations and repeats are common. One seven-minute film, *Hot Bagels*, has been shown on HBO over thirty times in a period of two years. Cable pays around $200 per minute for short films for a given period of a month or two. Despite this meager amount, cable has paid more money to independent filmmakers in the past five years than any other source.

We should take a moment to give some specifics about the money that can be made from films on television (about 75 percent of the revenue for short films).

In a survey made in 1983 of a variety of television stations across the country, I came up with the following figures. WGBH (Boston) pays $200 to $500 a half-hour for two screenings (fairly standard request). KQED (San Francisco) pays $5 per minute for a screening. WPBT (Miami) pays $200 per hour, WNET (New York) pays $1,000. WOUB (Athens, Ohio) pays $1 to $1.50 per minute, and HUHT (Houston) pays $200 to $250 per hour. For commercial prime time programming these figures can be as much as 100 times greater. But such figures mean you must work in conjunction with a network from the start.

Foreign Showings

Foreign payment for American independent films has been growing, and Europeans are often seen at film festivals acquiring releases for TV abroad. Japan and England (BBC-1 and 2 pay $3,500 per half-hour) are major buyers of American programming. Mexico spends less, $900 per half-hour, but buys large quantities. Canada pays $1,500 and West Germany between $4,000 and $5,000 per half-hour.

An irony for the independent distributor is that European sales for a short film can be higher than they are in the U.S. Television has caught on abroad, and the demand has outstripped the supply. Europeans, and Asians too, for that matter, are curious about what is going on here and enjoy the seeming honesty of the independently produced films they see. The Germans, for example, revel in films about social problems. They seem to take a perverse pleasure in films depicting racial problems and the dark side of the colossus across the Atlantic. European countries with their state-owned television stations are more likely to screen what we might call "fine art" in the U.S. PBS does allocate some time to this kind of work, which they might lump together as "avant garde," but even these supposedly noncommercial stations feel a pressure to satisfy the demands of the audience for entertainment. European countries usually pay a flat fee for a screening, around $2,000 per hour; if the film is popular, it could play in a dozen different stations.

Airing Your Work on Public Television

The public broadcasting stations around the country were once looked on as the salvation of the independent filmmaker, and, in fact, a few programs did turn that promise into fruition. Notable among them was "51st State," a "variety" program, for lack of a better term, that was produced by WNET, Channel 13, in New York City. This weekly program used many short films produced by independents and in so doing gave many young filmmakers a start in the business. The mid-1970's, when "51st State" flourished, was a golden age for makers of short films. Now, as you may have gathered, short film production is not a significant part of the film industry. Very few people make a living with short films, and those manage to survive only for brief periods before going into teaching or making commercials.

But for the beginner, the person who wants to break into features or commercials, the short film is an important stage of development. Not everyone can afford to reach into his pocket and produce a "Carte Visité," or show reel. So there needs to be some way of paying the cost of this education. Television, with its voracious appetite, is a likely candidate for that support; but television is a business, and a business faced with an abundance of "product" naturally takes advantage of the situation. Most stations do not have significant production crews; they simply buy material from short-film producers, and at the station's rates. The most likely buyers of short films are public broadcasting stations such as WNET, one of the major producing stations among the more than 260 across the country. The procedure for selling a film to any of these stations is much the same; following is the process that WNET uses to acquire material. Approximately half of the film projects at WNET are initiated by or in some way involve producers and filmmakers from the independent community.

To submit an idea you need the kind of material you would use to apply for a grant: a proposal, treatment, manuscript, or detailed outline and any audiovisual samples that can be submitted for evaluation. The Program Planning Department handles such proposals; they will look over the material and call you in for a meeting if the proposal reflects current priority needs and they think they can come up with the money.

If you have a finished film, it is another matter. In a recent year the Acquisitions Department at WNET screened over 225 films submitted by individual independents. Fifty-one of those films were acquired for local broadcast and paid for out of station discretionary funds. Station funds are also used to cover the costs of transferring each film to tape and paying for local promotion costs. Here it is a simple and quick process. Submit the completed film to the Acquisitions Department, and in ten days to two weeks you will get a decision. If they like the work they will negotiate terms and then issue a contract that specifies an air date. Rates average from $3 to $5 a minute, depending on rights negotiated, schedule placement, and program quality. If the film is scheduled for the Public Broadcasting System, national fees are negotiated between the filmmaker and the presenting station, in conjunction with PBS.

But whether it is local or national, remember that stations like WNET do not buy or own your production. They buy only the broadcast rights. Local broadcast rights are usually two "releases" in a two-year period. A release is usually a screening followed by another within a week. For films of less than a half-hour, the station will probably seek a multiple broadcast within a two- or three-year period. National broadcast rights are four releases within a three-year period, and, like the local arrangements, a release is restricted to a seven-day period.

All submissions are looked at by station engineers, who must certify the production as "broadcast" quality. The preferred format is 16mm with optical sound, and if the production has been carefully done there should be no problem in certifying it. PBS requires national programs to conform to standard lengths of 28 minutes, 58 minutes, or 88 minutes. If a program falls short, the station must find something to fill the time, and they would rather not go to the trouble. They are more likely to try to cut your work to bring it down to a shorter format. Such editing is often a bone of contention with filmmakers, and most people avoid it by conforming to the standard lengths. One advantage to the filmmaker is that WNET handles all transfers to video, so there is little additional cost when agreement is reached.

What to Expect from Commercial Distributors

Generally, three kinds of "deals" are prevalent in the distribution of 16mm shorts: outright sale, advance against percentage, and percentage only.

Outright sale is not as common as you might think; it is more prevalent when a distributor bids for American rights to foreign products. You know what you paid for your film, but can you put a price on your blood, sweat, and tears?

An advance is the same as "front money." Although the range goes from $500 to $15,000, $1,000 to $2,000 tends to be the standard. Only a minority of contracts signed involve an advance. Some distributors, as a point of policy, never pay front money; others always do; most pay only when they have to. When the advance matches the film's percentage earnings, royalty payments begin.

Percentage only is the most common arrangement offered currently. The filmmaker receives a flat percentage on all sales and rentals of his film, paid quarterly or semiannually. The percentage may be the same for sales and rentals, or the rental figure may be 5 or 10 points lower. Sometimes a sliding percentage is offered, with sales over a set number receiving an increased percentage.

Payments made on a percentage basis are called royalties, and they resemble royalties paid to writers by publishers and to performers by recording companies. Percentages currently paid by commercial distributors range from 17½ to the equivalent of 37½ percent, but the most common figures are 20 and 25 percent. Although these percentages seem low, they are generous when compared to royalties paid to writers and performers. When a distributor takes on a film, he must invest a certain amount in prints and promotion, and if the film doesn't sell, it's his loss.

Several other factors enter into the question of percentage offers. The company that pays only 17½ percent has fifteen salesmen in the field and thinks in terms of an initial run of 500 to 1,000 prints. Another company, much smaller and more specialized, pays the filmmaker on a 50/50 basis after the cost of the print—ordered individually, and at a higher price—is deducted. To the filmmaker, the question of percentage size is less important than what company can sell the most prints.

Since percentage deals depend upon actual sales and rentals of the film, and since it takes a distributor time to launch a new title—to have prints made, to put it in his catalog, to prepare a brochure—filmmakers should not expect big earnings immediately. Most important, if the film generates little interest among buyers, the filmmaker can expect little income. If it does well, he can expect healthy earnings paid on a regular basis.

Generally, the larger distributors insist on exclusive contracts, that is, the exlusive right to sell and rent 16mm prints of a film to schools, libraries, and film societies. If they decide to subdistribute your film, that's their right and business, but the filmmaker may not do any distribution on his own or through other companies (television, theatrical, and small-gauge format deals excluded, since these are often dealt with separately).

Some smaller companies offer (or insist upon) nonexclusive contracts, allowing the filmmaker to supplement distribution on his own or through other outlets. Occasionally a distributor who usually takes on only exclusive products will agree to a nonexclusive contract, but only if he badly wants the film in question.

Some distributors also ask for "other" rights. Those include theatrical rights, the hardest market of all for the short film. Most distributors won't even try, and most don't even mention the word.

Some distributors pay higher percentages for television bookings (national, local, public, and commercial); if the TV rights are already tied up, this is seldom a stumbling block.

Small-gauge formats—discs, tapes, Super-8 cartridges—are a subject of considerable confusion and speculation in the industry. Few actual attempts at this kind of marketing for shorts have been made. Many distributors ask for the rights but don't know what, if anything, they'll do with them.

Contracts are generally for five years, for seven years, or for "perpetuity." Some distributors like to give themselves an option to renew.

Distributors, of course, don't want to be sued and may insist that the filmmaker take care of potential problems. Are you the sole owner of your film? If it was made on a grant or in partnership with someone else, are there strings attached to your freedom to distribute it? Do you have releases from people in your film? Have you investigated music rights?

Sources of Revenue

Lets review for a moment all the sources of revenue for an independently produced short film. Documentary, drama, animation, or experimental, all can potentially get revenue from rentals of prints, sales of prints to libraries and schools, and broadcast by both domestic and foreign television. A popular film such as *Hiroshima/Nagasaki* produced by Erik Barnouw can sell over a thousand prints, show on fifty television systems, and get a hundred rentals a year for ten years. Relative to the cost of the average short film, this is a return greater than box-office hits like *Star Wars*. Unfortunately, the majority of the two hundred to three hundred short films made in the U.S. each year do not even make their cost. A well-done film on a popular subject can expect to sell twenty to thirty prints, be screened on several cable sytems, bring in fifty rentals the first year, and be shown on four foreign television systems.

Lets translate the average production's popularity into money. Assume that the film is twenty-eight minutes long, in 16mm color, and appropriate for screening on television. Each print costs $150 in lab charges and can be sold for around $500. That is a profit of $350 for each print sold, about $8,000 to $9,000 total. The cable systems may provide $10,000 to $15,000 in total. Rentals at about $60 per screening can bring in another $2,000 over a period of two years. If the film is not heavily dependent on colloquial English and is appropriate for a foreign audience, another $8,000 can be added to the projected revenue. That brings the total to about $30,000.

There are no guarantees that a half-hour film will make this kind of money, but if there is a proven demand for the information in the film and you have presented it in a professional manner, it is well within the realm of probability. Most of the films that fail to earn this kind of revenue were not thoroughly researched; that is, the filmmakers failed to find out if there was a demand for the film before they began. During the recent upsurge in women's issues, every film on or related to women's rights, problems in the job market, or being a single parent was snapped up, and several second-rate films were put in the limelight and made a lot of money. Of course, it is hard to predict social trends, but if you think like a stockbroker your chances of making it in the long run will increase.

You can say to yourself after this conservative, practical advice that James Joyce never did a market analysis, and Hemingway was never concerned about the sale of his books, and you would be right. Where would we be without somebody willing to take chances? I would be the last person to try to dissuade someone from following his instincts or convictions in making a film. Just keep in mind that the only production cost Hemingway had was a $200 typewriter and Joyce avoided even that by writing with a pencil. The total cost of all the paint Jackson Pollock used in his lifetime was undoubtedly less than the average cost of a short film. Filmmakers deal with sizable sums of money, and with that money comes responsibility. One of the first things a producer asks about a director is whether he is bankable, that is, whether he is capable of working under a given budget. The same criterion holds even at the documentary level, so it is important to discuss what a film like the one we have described can cost.

Production Costs

The rule of thumb in the 1960's was to estimate the cost of a documentary at $1,000 per minute. Adjusted for inflation, we come up with a figure of $1,500 per minute for the 1980's, and when all is said and done it remains a reasonable figure to use as a guide. It includes all salaries, film stock, transportation, rentals, and laboratory costs up to the final print. What should be striking about this $1,500 figure is that a half-hour production will cost more than we have estimated it can make. That should make it clear why so few short noncommercial films are made on speculation: by putting up personal capital and hoping to make it back. Unless the film is exceptional, it is likely to lose money.

Any film has three categories of expense: the salaries or fees of the people working on it; the production costs, which include equipment and film; and the laboratory costs. Cutting those costs can help to make a project more viable, and the first category that is usually cut is salaries. Actors and crew will often work diligently for a share of the profits of the film. This is done by assigning "points." Each film has 100 points, each of which represents 1 percent of the net profit from the production. A cameraman might receive five points, an actor two. This system is usually supplemented by an agreement that the salaries that would have been earned are paid out of the first profits from the production. The reason for this is that the "net" is an elusive figure. The gross income, or all the money that the film makes, is easy to figure out. The net is the amount left after all the expenses associated with the production are deducted. To say the least, this is a most elusive figure in Hollywood, where lavish parties are considered as promotion and lawyers rule. But if you know the people involved and it benefits you as a beginner in the business, taking a percentage makes sense.

The two other areas of expense are less easy to cut. The equipment for 16mm productions is easily rentable anywhere in the country, and with the increased use of video, used cameras are being sold at very reasonable prices. This has resulted in a secondary market of people willing to undercut the traditional rental prices and sometimes also take a share in the success of the production. Laboratories may also be willing to give an extended line of credit to someone with a worthy project. In other words, they do the processing and printing without demanding payment and then hold the negative as collateral for the outstanding charges. They usually let you have access to the finished product long enough to sell it, but if it isn't sold, it is filed away until the bill is paid.

I mention these financial details because most beginners in filmmaking start by making a film for their reel without a sponsor. It helps if that production shows a professional touch with high production values. Obviously you should seek out a good group to work with and decide what specific role you want to play in the production. Settle on the actual credit listing before starting anything. Remember that if all else fails, that will be your principal benefit. Also remember that a sample of your work must be the best you can do. People don't want to hear excuses when assessing the quality of someone's work.

The Association of Independent Video and Filmmakers (AIVF)

If you have made a firm decision to produce a film on your own, it is often a good idea to get together with others who have made the same decision and are trying to survive in the business.

The AIVF was founded for that purpose in 1974, with 125 charter members. Its ranks have tripled, and its magazine, *The Independent*, is the best single publication for the independent filmmaker in the country, carrying out the association's goal of keeping all filmmakers informed and up-to-date. The AIVF is a service organization of and for moving-image artists and craftspeople. It came into being through a grant from the U.S. Office of Education.

The AIVF has regularly monthly meetings at which members' films and videotapes are screened and presentations are given on such topics as screening outlets, theatrical distribution, self-distribution, and problems encountered in producing and directing.

The principles of the association center on providing practical, informational, and moral support, encouraging "diversity of vision," and lobbying for the acceptance of independent film and video as "valuable and vital expressions of our culture." For more about AIVF activities, contact them at 625 Broadway, New York, where they keep a well-stocked library containing much more advice about getting started in this complex business than I can cram into this book.

Chapter **III**

Marketing

"...a motion picture is the only commodity that does not carry an established price tag..."

M.J.E. McCarthy

We have discussed in general the production of different types of films, the kind of people who work on them, and getting started in films.

The one common denominator in our discussion has been money, something few filmmakers ever get enough of. A painter can work for years with few expenses: Paint and canvas can't be compared to $65 for ten minutes of 16mm color film, which is doubled in development and tripled in printing. Raising money for a film is the prinipal job of producers, from Otto Preminger to D.W. Griffith.

Features

If you were to look for a definition of a feature film producer, "businessman" might fit as well as any; a businessman who understands how films are made. This understanding need not extend to involvement in production or the aesthetic questions that arise in making films. In fact, a good producer is smart to distance himself from the "art" of the movies; it helps to maintain the objectivity that is a proven plus for producers. The moguls who put Hollywood on the map were selling furs and real estate one year; in the next, they were making pictures for profit. The same principles applied. Aside from a few high rollers such as Francis Ford Coppola, the principal objective of today's producers is to raise money, minimize risk, and maximize profit.

The producer is the least likely to get hurt if a production runs into trouble and the most likely to make money. After all, that's why he is in it. He isn't an artist looking for a chance to express himself.

To the beginner, this means that if you are interested in being a producer you will have to be good with money. A lot of it passes through a production very quickly, and the ability to economize without compromising the production is often the difference between showing a profit or declaring a loss. The financial details are too complex to go into here except to say that producers of features are world-famous for shady dealing. That is not to say that they make deals illegally. They have a lawyer right by their side as they steal you blind. Of course, they really don't steal from you; they only try to, and it is up to you to see that they don't. To gain this kind of savvy you have to work in the business and have a cautious nature. No school has more than a course or two in film business; it has to be learned on the job.

Producers do take risks, but usually with other people's money, and they write the contracts to cover themselves as well as possible in case of failure. A crew member stays with it and stands to profit if the film becomes popular. If it is not popular, it can be quickly dumped and as much written off as possible, with the producer moving on to the next project.

Distributors

It often costs more to get a picture properly advertised than it does to make it. This means that the staff for marketing and promoting a film is actually larger than the production crew. It can also be as creative and as important to the film's success.

Distributors are the link between the producer and the theater owner. Most of what they do is advertising. They need to assess the potential of the film, figure out how to accentuate those points, and release it.

Lets take, for example, a small (one million-dollar budget) production done in 1984, *Silent Madness*. Several wealthy businessmen in Washington decided to invest in a film and approached a New York company, August Films, for a script. August came up with one that fit the backers' profile, lined up a few name actors, among them Viveca Lindfors and several soap opera actors, and planned for a release in the summer. They set a six-week production schedule and set out to make what would have been called a few years ago a "B" movie. The story line was a simple chase with a few twists based on ideas from successful recent films, proven situations that will work as straightforward entertainment for some people and as satire for the "in" crowd.

After the shooting script was written, it was cast through notices in *Backstage* and *Variety*. Hundreds showed up to audition for the parts listed as "sorority girl," "deranged killer," and "small-town sheriff." When the cast was signed up and the technical crew assembled, everyone traipsed across the East River to Jersey City, where the city had donated an abandoned hospital to the production. Here the sets were constructed for half the scenes in the film; artificial blood was made from glycerine, food coloring, and starch; and the special-effects people started making fake limbs that would be chopped off in the half-dozen grisly episodes that are sprinkled throughout the plot.

For the next month and a half, with occasional forays to the outside for a scene or two, the crew of forty filmmakers lived in that hospital, eating on the top floor, moving the equipment from room to room for separate scenes. Some slept right at the location; others took the regular shuttle bus that was run between New York and Jersey City. The days were long, and tempers ran short after working in cramped hot corridors for twelve hours a day, six days a week.

The producer-writer of this film was William Milling, and the director was Simon Nuchtorn. Bill would comb through the wreckage of the building trying to find interesting areas in which to shoot scenes, while Simon would run through each scene with the actors. One of the things that strike you on a set like the one for *Silent Madness* is the quantity of physical labor involved in building sets and lighting them. Miles of cable are laid, gallons of paint applied—a few minutes of shooting and it is all torn down and reassembled elsewhere. The gaffers and the grips are more important than most people realize. More and more Hollywood films are being made on location, that is, outside the sound stages. A set can easily be constructed in a sound stage: Flats are swung over and joined, the prop room comes up with the appropriate furniture, and lights are swiveled into place. On

Rehearsing a scene from Silent Madness, Solly Marx practices one of the many murders he is called on to commit as a mad killer mistakenly released from a mental hospital. (Victim is Katie Bull.)

location someone has to find real furniture, lights have to be mounted with elaborate brackets, and each scene has to be carefully plotted out so that there will be room for the camera to get a good shot. On a sound stage all one need do is remove a wall to locate the camera, and the lights are mounted on a grid of pipes where the ceiling normally would be. One advantage to the producer on a remote location is that it is a lot easier to use nonunion labor, at a saving of nearly 50 percent. This shoot was a mixture of union and nonunion workers, which is typical for low-budget features and makes such films ideal for a young filmmaker learning the trade. Getting to know union people can help also, because they can be sponsors or references when the time comes to apply for membership.

When *Silent Madness* finally "wrapped," it was a week behind schedule because the 3-D system designed by Arriflex failed to work for a while, but it was within the budget. The cast and crew threw a final party and scattered to other projects while Simon took the film into the editing room. About four months later the film was ready to be shown to a distributor.

Since the film was designed from the start as a salable "product," finding a distributor was not hard for August Films. At the first screening of the film, to which only the cast and crew were invited, Simon introduced it by saying, "I hope noboby came tonight expecting to see art; it is what it is." To the assembled filmmakers this premiere was a chance to sit back and enjoy the results of their labor. Every time they see the film, memories of the people and places will come back to them. That

The first of three posters for Silent Madness.

is one of the reasons they do what they do, and it is one of the things that has always fascinated me with the film profession. When you see a film you have worked on, you are struck by the difference between what you know happened and the surreal new world that the film creates.

To a distributor the film is simply a product to be marketed. It is the distributor's job to know how to get the film out to theaters. A good distributor combs through *Variety* weekly, studying the statistics, looking for trends. The film mentioned earlier, *He Knows You're Alone*, was popular because a similar film, *Friday the 13th*, was setting box-office records at the time. The distributor simply rode the coattails of the earlier film and copied the marketing strategy.

A distributor takes the responsibility for the film, leaving the producer free to work on other projects. The distributor for *Silent Madness* had a lot of decisions to make. For one, the film had been shot in 3-D, and just before its completion another 3-D film had been released and had bombed. Now the distributor had to decide whether it was the quality and content of the film that made it fail, or whether the 3-D process itself was the problem. The distributor also faced the problem of how to release the film. If it were sneaked in through a few theaters at a low cost, it could develop a reputation through word of mouth. It could also be killed by the critics. If a large number of prints, at high cost, were sent out in a blitz, with heavy advertising, the film might get a good audience through curiosity alone. The critics wouldn't have time to kill it at the box office. At this point in time *Silent Madness* has not yet been released. It is scheduled for summer 1985.

Distributors are gamblers. They buy a film in the hope that they can sell it for a profit. During the 1930's and 1940's distribution was handled by the studios that made the films, but today most films are both produced and distributed by so-called independent companies. Look closely at the credits the next time you go to the movies. Often three or four companies are listed, whereas years go it was simply an RKO or a Universal picture and everybody from the writer to the producer worked for that company.

Concentrating the industry in a handful of large companies

made it easy to know where to look for a job. A beginner today can be confused by the array of companies, many of which are only names or temporary divisions of other companies. Sorting them out can be made a bit easier by checking *The Hollywood Reporter*, *Variety*, and *Backstage* for word of who is planning to go into production, where and when. These periodicals keep track of the industry, almost like a newsletter for the fraternity of filmmakers. You will notice as you read them that the major productions discussed in the tabloids and the cultural landmarks discussed in the Sunday New York *Times* are only a small segment of the industry. A lot of "potboilers" like the films we have discussed are being made, a lot of commercials, and more industrial and corporate films than most people realize. When you read of a production beginning, remember that six to eight weeks later it will go into post-production and in less than a year it will be in the hands of a distributor, who will hire as many people and spend as much money as the producer did to get the finished product out to the audience.

Distributors will soon face a major change in the way films are marketed. Videocassettes have become enormously popular in a few short years. Some industry watchdogs predict that rentals and sales of VHS and Betamax cassettes will be a major source of revenue for many different types of films. For example, a 16mm production entitled *The Other Side of Nashville* bypassed theaters, television, and even cable TV to premiere in the summer of 1984 as a videocassette. A documentary on country music with several well-known performers, it cost over $250,000 and was originally intended for broadcast television. MGM made the decision to release it first as a cassette thinking that country fans would want to collect it as a behind-the-scenes look at their favorite performers. It sold 10,000 copies in the first month. I mention these developments because the easiest entry points in any profession are at the points where it is changing. Nobody can question your experience, and it is often easier to train someone on the job than to retrain someone.

The current feature film business is dominated by fewer than ten distributors. Companies such as Warner, Universal, MGM, Paramount, and 20th Century-Fox produce, distribute, and exhibit. All these companies have changed radically over the years, by diversifying or merging, but they have held onto a great deal of the structure and expertise that provide power in the marketing and advertising of major motion pictures, the budgets of which have been growing steadily over the past decade. The Motion Picture Association of America (MPAA) represents these major companies along with a few other "mini-majors" in their dealings with courts, exhibitors, and the public. The majors own approximately thirty offices nationwide in order to distribute films.

Most of the ample coverage of the film field concentrates on the artistic end: film's auteurs. Little is said about the great gray bulk of the profession: the marketing of movies. The business is divided into three areas: the majors (and mini-majors like Embassy and Cannon) doing the majority of the work; independent companies, mostly financed by these distributors; and finally independent production companies operating on their own. The majority of these companies are short-lived; most only last long enough to make one to five films.

Exhibition is even more concentrated, with four companies controlling over 500 screens and one (General Cinema) with more than 900. There are fewer than 35 circuits with 50 to 100 screens. This concentration of power is recent. Until the 1960's there were thousands of independent movie houses (remember *The Last Picture Show*?) spread across the country. Today there are some 5,000 independent theater owners with one to ten screens. Some major changes are likely in the near future. High-definition television coupled with a good projection system may move exhibitors away from film altogether. Eastman Kodak studies show that this is not imminent, however. What is more likely to be the imminent threat to the current system is the humble videocassette. With nearly five million VCRs in homes across the country, and several thousand film titles available for rental, the videocassette is what theater owners fear most.

I mentioned earlier that the entire film industry is small. One figure is worth remembering. In 1980 there were 213,000 people working in the film business, and that figure grows at a rate of 5 percent per year. I would venture to say that two out of three of those people work in distribution and marketing—the less glamorous end. As in many professions, the people who make the product are often very different from the people who sell it. If you have ever been to an "opening" for an artist, you understand what I mean. Customers, collectors, critics, and gallery owners mill about while the hapless artist sits back isolated by the occasion. The drive to create films is an artistic drive that is difficult for salesmen to comprehend, even though they make their living from that creative impulse.

The best illustration of creativity was made by Saul Bass in his short film *Why Man Creates*, which should be seen by every aspiring filmmaker. It is this spark that is the heart of this industry. All the moguls and their megabuck deals are as nothing without somebody able to turn a spark of creativity into a work of art. The kindling for the spark comes from producers and distributors, and thus an "odd couple" is formed: one person driven by an "irrational" impulse to create and the other driven by the desire to accumulate more capital.

The last film that I shot and co-produced was *The Other Side of Nashville*, and the distributors, MGM, recently invited me to the opening of the film in New York. When I walked into the suite where the film would be shown in an hour, the rooms were packed with well-dressed young people all wolfing down a chicken dinner, drinking, and talking up a storm. It struck me that very few people really cared much about the movie they were to see. Of course the evening did finally get around to that point, and the lights were dimmed for the MGM representative to make his introduction. The executive chosen for this inaugural screening was a middle-aged man who would have looked at home in a Cadillac showroom touting the latest Fleetwood. He stood up and proceeded to explain how MGM had recognized the impact of country-western music and gone out to make this film, etc.—when in fact all they had done was put up a small amount of completion money for a distribution deal when the film was already in the can. Even though the entire crew who shot the film were present, not a single one was introduced.

The incident was fairly typical. The businessmen who run the marketing companies are reluctant to acknowledge the creators, partly because they don't fully understand what it is that drives them, and partly because they want people to know that they are the ones in control: Only if *they* choose to handle the film will it see the light of day. To them discovering an artist or filmmaker is the important process, because we all know how many of these poor souls are out there waiting to come in from the cold.

Film critic Pauline Kael bluntly states, "The businessmen have always been in control of film production; now advertising puts them finally on top of public reaction as well. They can transcend the content and quality of a film by advertising." Kael comes down on producers, also, "In no other field is the entrepreneur so naked a status-seeker. Underlings are kept busy arranging awards and medals for the producer, whose name looms so large in the ads that the public—and often the producer himself—comes to think he actually made the picture. Ross Hunter, Robert Radnitz, even Hal Wallis in recent years hardly have room in the advertising for the writers' and directors' names. In many cases their pictures fail because they insist on employing nonentity directors who don't assert any authority."

Kael, from her long acquaintance with the industry, feels that producers resent artists: cameramen, directors, and so on. She feels that producers hate "ungovernable" artists and resent their fame as if they represented a privileged class of people who don't have to stoop to the kind of things a producer does to make a film. The moneymen in the Hollywood movie scene feel that the artist's crime is caring less for profits than for his art. Producers are often heard complaining about directors who want to try "something different." To the producers such ideas are self-destructive, irresponsible. Artists in Hollywood are often ridiculed by producers. Those that "toe the line" are artists with discipline. If a maverick makes a film that proves popular, he is an outcast; in fact, producers enjoy seeing such a person fail. Kael feels that in the ongoing battle between the artists and the producers, the artists are outfoxed nearly every time.

Businessmen spend a lot of time and energy in strategy and manipulation to maintain that dominance. One classic bone of contention is the right of final cut. This control over the editing of the film is a symbol of how the industry permits producers "to play God with other people's creations," often resulting in a mangled mess that is blamed, of course, on the director. Artists are simply no part of the producer's team; they don't get protection.

When films enter the sphere of television, the control of the producer is even greater. With the smaller budgets, there is less time for production and more compromise in the trip from script to tube. A dedicated movie buff bemoans the TV movies' lack of visual beauty, spatial sense, and fusion of image and sound. TV movies are paced to get you quickly into the story before you reach the dial; they usually do well in developing character and tension, but rarely does beauty come into the picture. Pauline Kael feels that TV movies are not movies at all, but TV programs retrieved through a device that is another piece of furniture.

Kael feels that television represents what happens to a medium "when the artists have no power and the businessmen are in full unquestioned control." The medium of film has not abandoned its artists, who are still putting out work that has nothing to do with marketing analysis, but only with the artist's personal conviction. If films are to remain powerful and influential, we need such commitment. Artists must be given the opportunity to give their utmost "even if the audience shows every sign of preferring something easy, cheap and synthetic."

Documentaries

We have pretty well covered the way documentaries are sold, but a few points are worth underscoring. Documentaries have a much smaller market than do features, and quite often it is hard to find a company willing to distribute a production. Many filmmakers have simply taken over the distribution of their own work, with good results. This direct approach has given rise to cooperatives that help the individual by storing and mailing the film to customers. The best known are the Canyon Cinema Cooperative in San Francisco and the New York Coop. These are nonprofit organizations of independent filmmakers who banded together to create a catalog and an inexpensive way to get their films out to libraries and museums. It is a bit like a group of painters deciding to take the power away from the galleries and opening their own. The weakness in this concept is that since it is a cooperative there is no way to assure the quality of the work being distributed. A gallery owner selects what will be shown, but in a co-op everything is listed. The lack of quality control hurt the co-ops, but fortunately there was enough solid criticism from film festivals so that people could separate the good from the bad, and the co-ops are still alive, although not exactly thriving.

The difficult thing to get across about documentaries and short films is that to do them you must be part artist and part entrepreneur. There are very few jobs per se out there, and when it comes to distribution the world will not beat a path to your door to look at your latest production. It is a business in which contacts are everything; you must get to know as many people as possible. The film business is concentrated in major cities, and people take every opportunity to go to screenings, to be seen busy (if possible), and to keep up the contacts they have made. Try to do favors for people, help them out without pay when they need it, see them socially, find out who are the important people and let them know of your interest—repeatedly, if necessary. Persistence pays off. Positions are usually filled by personal recommendation, not by a personnel official looking over an application form. People who get you a job on a shoot want to know how you respond to overtime, whether you are reliable, whether you have the skills and can get along with a variety of people under pressure. The only way you can show these traits is to get out and demonstrate them. Start doing favors, and before long those favors will be returned.

Chapter IV

Industrial/Educational Films

"The business of America is business."

Calvin Coolidge

A large share of the film business lies in producing for corporations. A company may want to show how a new product works or document a test of its durability. It may have a problem training the staff to use a forklift truck, or its salesmen may need tips on techniques for selling a new product. Not especially exciting stuff, but it can be a good living. As corporations grow, sometimes becoming international, their need for "communication" increases. One branch needs to tell other branches what it is up to, annual reports are increasingly being filmed or taped instead of printed, and ready access anywhere in the world to video tape recorders to retrieve the programs has spurred the use of motion pictures in corporate circles.

Larger corporations have their own audiovisual departments. These are small for the most part, with a television camera, a recorder, and an area to do interviews that one might call a studio. These facilities belie the substantial budgets for media. Corporations shy away from having a large permanent staff with the need for retirement benefits, health insurance, and so on. They farm out most of their work to independent film and video producers, who bid on specific projects. This enables the company to avoid the costly benefits associated with permanent employees while giving it access to a wide selection of producers with specific talents and skills. For example, a company might need underwater photography or animation, but it would be wasteful to keep specialists or equipment around unless they were used regularly.

Working on industrial or corporate films takes on the coloration of the business world. Efficiency, reliability, and professionalism are the key attributes. Creativity is not as high on the list of desirable traits as in other branches of film production. A documentarian is expected to be politically critical and liberal, an animator creative but immersed in aesthetic considerations, and the feature filmmaker willing to sell his soul to the devil for a smash hit with his name in lights, but the corporate media person is somewhat colorless. Many people who started out in the more colorful areas of film are now working in industrials. Francis Thompson, whose classic avant-garde film *N. Y, N. Y.* helped to bring film to the attention of the art establishment, is now working for railroad companies. The Maysles brothers who shot *Salesmen* and *Cristo's Valley Curtain* (well-received documentaries) are now doing commercials. The point is not that these people sold out, but rather that they changed: Their needs changed. In my own work I have turned from creative projects to commercial work because I have children to put through college.

In starting out, an easy way to get a salaried job is to learn the technical side of media. Technicians and engineers are in great demand today. Keep in mind that there is a reason for the shortage of qualified technicians. Video has burst upon the scene, and with it a new and complex technology. The people doing the hiring for these positions need people who understand the intricacies of TV hardware, slide controllers, and film equipment. In fact, it can be said of everybody in the business that versatility is the key to success. Sometimes it proves more effective or less expensive to do a slide presentation than to commit a project to motion-picture film. Most companies have small permanent departments to deal with media, and the more versatile a person is, the better, particularly now that we appear to be undergoing a shift to stereo ½-inch cassettes and broadcast TV, to videodisc, to a magnetic coding system for film (datacode), and to computer controls for multiple-slide presentations.

Very few people today refer to their position in a company as film specialist or film producer: They are media specialists or media producers. The best people in these positions usually have been trained in film, but their skills are not limited to film. Jessica Fish, media producer for Hughes Aircraft in Los Angeles, says: "There are a lot of advantages to being a communications specialist. You should have some kind of knowledge of other production media and the new technologies, such as teleconferencing and interactive video." She goes on to summarize a common feeling: "Being a woman in corporate media means you have to walk a very fine line, but it's a lot more open to women than a lot of other professions."

That comment describes the potential for women in media in a nutshell. A large percentage of corporate media executives are women. It appears to be a popular position among women; and corporations, often seeking to balance historically lopsided hiring policies, actually seek women for many of these positions.

I should point out that production and technical people are mostly men. One reason for this is obvious: The heavy camera equipment requires an operator to have strength in the upper body. The additional equipment involved in shooting either film or video is also bulky, heavy, and apparently more than most women want to put up with. That may all change soon. The weight of a video camera in 1984 is one-quarter of what it was in 1978, and the decks are half as large. Film equipment has also become smaller, with miniature recorders and quartz lights taking the burden off production crews.

Government Projects

The largest single employer in the industrial or educational field is the federal government. Beginning with the dust-bowl film *The Plow That Broke the Plains*, produced during the depression by Pare Lorenz for the Department of Agriculture, the government has been making films. During World War II production reached a peak. Separate film units in the Army, the Navy, the USIA, and other agencies were turning out hundreds of short films a year. All but a few of those units have now been eliminated.

The government puts out bid requests every month to independent production companies, and hundreds of companies survive on these contracts. Unfortunately a lot of red tape is involved with the bids: multiple copies of everything, careful budgeting, and sworn compliance with laws regarding the environment, hiring of minorities, and so on. All that is to be expected from the federal bureaucracy, but it makes the bidding process long and difficult.

al_FILMS**   **73**

The government lets most of its contracts to film productions, but the short-term projects are usually done on television equipment. It is safe to predict that more and more work will be done on television equipment. Already there is a major shift in post-production to the use of video editing equipment. The emphasis has been on film because the quality of film cameras has been superior to that of video cameras. There is a good chance that the difference will narrow in the near future, and most technical personnel are preparing for the changeover.

School Production

The second-largest segment of this area of production belongs to schools. Every high school and college in the country has an audiovisual department. During the 1950's and 1960's most of the film processing labs in the country were kept profitable by developing 16mm film of football games. Most games are recorded on video today, but film production classes still use a lot of film. Film equipment is simpler, more durable, and less expensive than video, and so it remains popular for beginning classes. The departments that teach film need technicians to keep everything working and check it out to students. The advantage of a position like this, which can be good for a beginner, is that the summers are very slow and provide a lot of spare time for personal projects. Audiovisual departments usually keep busy around the year. Colleges have especially large inventories of media gear, not just for instruction, but for research as well.

The person who finds it easy to adapt to school employment usually is patient and enjoys a relaxed environment enough to put up with a low salary. Colleges find it easy to get media employees. It is an interesting field, and there are always graduates who have settled in and find it convenient to hang on for a while before braving the cold world outside.

In years gone by, colleges, through their media centers or film units, were major producers of short films. Many documentaries and instructional films came from producers such as the University of Wisconsin and Northwestern and Columbia Universities. The only films that come from colleges and universities today are those that are funded by outside grants, or those that promote the school. A good way to check up on this kind of work is to join the University Film and Video Association, which publishes a *Journal* and holds an annual meeting in August on a college campus. To get a look at the scope of employment in academic areas, the Speech Communication Association has an excellent placement service that serves teachers and staff as well.

Just a note about applying for a job with any company. No matter what your eventual plans are, you can learn a lot by apprenticing or working for pay with an established company. This may be the best move for someone just out of college who is not tied to a career as an artist or independent filmmaker. The general guidelines for applying for a job are the same as for most fields: Be clear in outlining your career objectives, brief, courteous, and show that you can write by sending the prospective employer a letter both before and after the interview.

As in any profession, you need a résumé. This may only be glanced at, but don't ignore its potential. If you don't make it on the first round, that résumé will be in the file waiting to remind someone of who you are and what you can do. Be sure it is up-to-date and succinct. Skim your formal education and concentrate on your experience, and try to have a reel to demonstrate that experience.

It will probably be necessary to be persistent (film people are usually up to their ears in work or potential work) and have the confidence in yourself to put up with the inevitable rejections.

Finding a job can be the hardest job you will ever have. Put all the energy into your search and applications that you would put into the job itself. Keep in mind that there are 250,000 people out there who found a slot and are working in film; there is no reason why you can't be one of them.

Film Schools

Starting in the mid-1960's, schools began to realize the importance of the popular arts, including cinema. At first colleges were reluctant to adopt film study along with the more traditional disciplines, partly out of concern lest it become too popular and divert students from the rigors of learning grammar, languages, and so on. As it turned out, the fears of English and foreign-language professors were real: Film engulfed higher education. Within ten years film spread from three or four schools to nearly every college and university in the country. This buildup peaked around 1980. Any current growth in the size of film departments is in the areas of television, videodisc, and general study of media in our society. The film study has not retreated, only retrenched to fit more comfortably with the newer electronic technologies, which often involve computers. Most people agree that a good college program is the best first step toward a career in film.

The appendix lists some of the best schools to consider, either as a student or as a job applicant if you are interested in working in higher education. A later chapter discusses the prospects for teaching film.

One note of caution worth repeating: The teachers you find in high school and college have probably never worked in "the business." To qualify as a college teacher, you must spend so much time in school that it is almost impossible to gain any practical experience. Some schools, such as New York University, UCLA, and Ithaca College, hire people with professional backgrounds, but most are concerned only with degrees and publications. As film grew, some schools were forced to transfer professors from other departments, such as English, into film departments because they had tenure and could not be let go.

If you are interested in production, it is not really essential to go to college. In fact, a degree can almost be a handicap, since the unions are largely made up of people who did not go to college. But if you are an aspiring director, it is a must. There is no other way to get an organized look at the influential films from the past. Film school graduates such as George Lucas and Steven Spielberg make constant references in their work to films that have influenced them. But the chance that the person sitting next to you in film class will be another Lucas or Spielberg is pretty remote. It is far more likely that the person is there because he likes films or is simply curious as to how they are made.

Most film programs are "liberal arts" oriented, with very little concern for the profession. There is a lot of discussion about theory and the creative process, and the pragmatic aspects are only touched on. There is nothing wrong with that as long as you know that you will still need to learn the pragmatic aspects of the business after graduation. It is unfortunate that most schools can't train a rounded professional, but that is a natural consequence of trying to incorporate film study with traditional disciplines, which are quite different in nature. Most countries look at film study as a separate field in need of governmental support to be effective. The model for most of the world is the Moscow Film School, which provides four intensive years of study fully underwritten by the government. This type of school also exists in Lodz, Poland, where Roman Polanski studied, and Prague, Czechoslovakia, where Milos Forman and Ivan Passer studied.

Just keep in mind, as you work your way through a film program, that eventually you will have to do some specific task. Try to concentrate on what that task will be and what you need to know to accomplish it. Having a direction at an early stage is the single most valuable trait anyone can have. If you find later that you would like to change to another area—from editing to cameraman, for example—it will be easier then. Don't expect too much from career guidance in college. They will give you a good idea of what constitutes a valuable film, teach you something about the nature of the medium, and—it is hoped—create an atmosphere in which your creativity will be nurtured. If you are a creative person, don't miss an opportunity to make a film. If your film demonstrates that you understand the nature of the medium, how to tell a story and touch people's emotions, it could be the most valuable thing you get out of school.

The Sponsored Film

There are a multitude of ways to put together or package the funding for a film. Successful filmmakers are skilled in locating people with money to spend and inventive in finding a way for them to spend it. One of the best ways to get support for a film is not through money at all, but through goods and services. Companies can write off all expenses involved with advertising. An airline, for example, could give you a standby ticket to shoot a film in Alaska. The airline need not spend a dime, but it will be able to deduct the value of your trip from its taxes. Since the airline is ahead of the game simply by giving you the ticket, it is less demanding than the typical backer who is looking for a profit on his investment. If you include a shot of the airline's planes in your film, it will probably suffice.

These "sponsored" films represent a good way for a beginner to raise money for a film. Some films are made entirely through the advertising budgets of a string of companies. Say, for example, you are interested in making a film on boating in Alaska. You would approach manufacturers of boats, fishing rods, binoculars, and vehicles, as well as airlines and show how their product or service would appear in the film, providing a subtle kind of advertising. Sales departments know that if a fifty-pound salmon is seen landed with a Penn reel, people are impressed in a way that can't be purchased with advertising. Many films are made this way with a patchwork of financial and product support written off as advertising. The resultant film usually remains the property of the producer, and he sells prints to his sponsors, among others.

Principal among those others are television stations with a need for inexpensive programs for "filler" during hours when the number of people watching is low. If the sponsored film is done in such a way that it is not obvious advertising, it can get hundreds of screenings. Modern Talking Pictures is a company that specializes in finding stations to air such sponsored films.

Even films that are commercial entertainment take advantage of the fact that the visibility of a product, from a car to a brand of bubble gum, is a subtle form of advertising and therefore worth something to the maker of that product. You can be sure that the production company does not pay for Burt Reynolds' souped-up car.

I mention this sidelight of the business to underscore the wide range of work that is tangential to filmmaking. A production crew is only the tip of the iceberg. It is these "unseen" jobs—placing a manufacturer's products in films and managing those props, placing films on television, and other unglamorous tasks—that make up the bulk of the accessible jobs in the film business. These are also jobs that make good entry-level positions.

It is worth pausing here to point out that there is a lot of room in the film business for entrepreneurs; in short, if you can't get someone to pay you a salary, turn the tables and make a job for yourself. The film and video companies that make most of the nonfeature-length productions in the U.S. are small, often only a husband-and-wife team like Susan and Alan Raymond, who did *An American Family* for Public Broadcasting. Even the distribution companies of nontheatrical films are small. ICAP, mentioned earlier as a leading distributor of short films to television, has only a few employees, and director Kitty Morgan knows most of her filmmakers personally. In an atmosphere like that it is relatively easy to find a service that you can perform. In the feature production business, where corporate thinking prevails, a person trying to carve out a business would find it difficult. Those small-business people I have seen carve out a niche for themselves have been in areas like catering (I admit that is a bit removed), equipment rental, transportation, research, and location scouting. I have known several filmmakers who got their start by looking for a company interested in renting equipment for a long period: They undercut the rental houses, signed a contract, got a loan, and bought the needed equipment. The equipment used in film is often a key to work. Since most of it is rented, one can buy a camera, recorder, or editing machine and rent it along with oneself. Even well-known filmmakers like the Mayseles brothers admit that they have been able to survive only through the rental of their equipment.

Distribution

The distribution of an educational film is crucial. Many a young filmmaker expects the world to beat a path to his door when he has finished a film. Even a film that has been researched, that is, for which there is proven need, requires a good push to get off.

I will assume that you have taken my advice and gone to college, emerging with a BA and a short film that you feel is good enough to go into distribution. Where do you turn? Without getting into details, the first place to go is a journal that will review it, like *Library Journal* or *Booklist*. Librarians, who are the largest buyers of short films, read these monthly journals regularly, and you can get requests for a film years after a review appears. These buyers usually contact the listed distributor, which, if you wish, can be yourself. They view the film and if they like it, buy it.

The next step is to submit to film festivals like the New York Independent Filmmaker's Exposition, the Sinking Creek Film Festival, or the American Film Festival. Here you might attract the interest of a distributor, win some prize money, and gain some constructive criticism.

Next you try to get a distributor to take on the film for both cable and film, sales and rentals. If you fail here, demand for your production is probably limited. But if you wish, you can continue on your own. Send out a descriptive flyer to people who might be buyers. A nonprofit organization in New York, Cine-Information, sells a mailing list of film buyers and users with specific interests, all cross-listed in its computer. After this, try one of the several brokers who supply films to foreign television. Still failing, hold onto the negative in a safe place and go on to other things. Take the best parts for a sample reel of your work and don't look back.

Miscellaneous Productions

Technology is changing. Film, still popular as a production medium, is now being abandoned when it comes to distribution, so it is important to understand the virtues and weaknesses of the various visual media in use today.

Videodisc. Despite the fact that the videodisc plays back through a television monitor, the original imagery from which it is mastered was most likely film. Film has a "resolution," or an ability to render detail, that is hard to match with videotape. The unique aspects of the videodisc—its interactivity, for one—make it an important technology to watch for the future. Since a disc can be accessed by a computer, understanding computer programming would also be a valuable skill to have.

The disc system that dominates the industry at this point is laser-activated and made mostly by Pioneer in Japan. Part of the slow growth in popularity of the videodisc was the result of a battle over which standard would prevail. Since the largest challenger to the laser system has folded (RCA closed the books on its system), growth should be steady. The disc will probably not be used extensively for popular films, as was the RCA disc, but the ability to call up an image or a sequence in a fraction of a second gives it enormous potential for archiving visual material and for training and sales. There is a good chance that home computers soon will use a type of videodisc in place of magnetic discs to store digital material.

The disc is a device for storage and retrieval of visual material, and as such it is a technology that librarians will be watching closely. That brings up another field that is as much a part of the film as those involved with production. Most libraries have collections of 16mm or 3/4-inch videocassettes, and it requires a substantial workforce to acquire and circulate those collections. Many of these people belong to the Educational Film Library Association and are trained as librarians with master's degrees in library science, A school like Syracuse University is a good choice, since it has both a strong library program and the Newhouse School of Communications on the same campus.

Animation. This is one corner of the film world that has not felt the impact of video. Efforts to do animation with video, such as the ill-fated Anavid, have all but disappeared. The field is highly specialized and not for everyone. A graphic artist with a theatrical flair might find it attractive, but it should be understood that the painstaking process of making a dozen or more drawings for each second of screen time can wear down the most patient soul. Many beginners gain a feel for the process and some actual credits by "inking" or filling in the color on the outlined acetate cells that are photographed to make the film. The California Institute of the Arts, funded with money from Walt Disney productions, and the Pratt Institute School of Art and Design are good schools for preparation as an animator. But remember, the job takes patience and perseverance.

Music Videos. Industry analysts predict that we may soon be buying videocassettes and discs of our favorite music just as we buy LPs today. To say the least, they have mushroomed in popularity, and there isn't a band around that hasn't at least contemplated making one.

On location making a "rock video" for CBS Records in Waltham, Massachusetts.

Despite the term "music video," almost all of these short musical productions are done on film. They have been a good format for beginning producers to get a start. Scripts are usually nil, being based on the lyrics of the music, and the products are all reasonably short and "glitzy," giving them high visibility in relation to the short production time. Despite these points in their favor, most of them make little or no money. The capital to produce them comes from the featured group or its record publisher and is looked upon as advertising expense. The MTV cable channel has taken advantage of this stockpile of free material to become a household word, and there has been talk of expanding from cable to video jukeboxes.

Most record companies view music videos as a necessary evil: to sell records. They put only enough money into them to get the musicians some exposure, so the profit margin for the producers of these short films is low. Still, it has been estimated that 1,200 original music videos were made in 1983 alone, and during that year record companies spent more than $50 million to produce them. The pace of production has not let up. In 1984 MTV reported that thirty-five music videos were being produced each week.

In an interview published in the New York *Times*, Mark Levinson, whose company Picture Music has turned out more than 150 music videos, said, "We see rock videos as just a springboard for a broader business . . . with the exposure we gained we did commercials for Coca-Cola, RCA, and Sony."

Larry Solters, vice president of MCA Records, is confident that the spots will continue to be made. "I just had a brilliant video produced for $20,000 by two unknown guys who were looking for a break. There are always going to be smaller companies who have no secretaries or business managers, who can do it for less." In the 1980's it appears almost mandatory for an aspiring director to do at least one of these short films, but it is unlikely that music videos will be a solid enterprise on which to base a career.

Short Films. Generally a short film is thought of as less than one hour in the U.S. and no longer than 40 minutes in Europe. Whatever the length or the type of films, the point is that they are not features. We have been talking about this nonfeature-length production through most of this book, because that is where many people begin their careers as producers, where they learn the ropes. Because these short films are being used in different ways today, however, I want to point out how understanding specific lengths can be useful.

With the advent of television in the 1950's, two original lengths for programs emerged, 27–30 minutes and 53–58 minutes, and it was foolhardy to ignore them. Television stations don't like to be bothered to find filler if a program does not end conveniently at the half-hour or the hour. Many producers learned the hard way that these lengths were important. It sometimes meant having to puff up a subject to reach a certain length or jettison a few details to get the program down to size. This restriction was looked on with disdain at first by filmmakers, who considered it just another example of corporate America calling the shots, usurping the individual artist's right to make an honest statement; but eventually it was adhered to or suffered in silence. Those who made short films always felt a little left out. The "feature" film system was where the power and the influence were. The 35mm scaled-down palaces were a part of the American scene, a conduit from Hollywood to Main Street America that was the envy of many short film producers because of its efficiency and financial success, but disliked by many for the escapist or socially irresponsible use of power. Most of the film artists and documentarians who rose up in the 1960's with their alternative to Hollywood disliked the aura of the movies. What they saw was a powerful tool that was going to waste, and they set about to show how it could be used to *deal* with society's problems, not just forget them.

What this new army of independents had in their favor was a television system with an insatiable appetite for programming. Robert Drew with D.A. Pennebaker and Ricky Leacock made history with some of the most insightful documentaries of the political process that have ever been made, following Hubert Humphrey about in *Primary*, and spending a day with John F. Kennedy. Television even extended its traditional boundaries to ninety minutes with several of these, and many believed that film had never been put to better use.

The early days of television were devoted to the broadcasting of film. As late as 1975, 80 percent of daytime programming was shot on film. To understand TV, you had to understand film. But in 1967 the Japanese, working with a series of American patents, began to export television cameras and recorders. Less than twenty years later, film as a production medium has all but disappeared from television. Of course, much of what TV broadcasts is still shot on film, but the news and TV documentaries that are done by the stations themselves are video. The last holdout among the networks is "60 Minutes" on CBS.

The Future: Video vs. Film

There is confusion in the eyes of beginning students of film these days. "What is happening in video?" they ask. "A technical revolution," I answer, "but nothing to worry about at this point, the basics haven't changed."

There is no question that the technology of motion pictures is changing; some are calling this the era of "electronic cinema." Each year we increase our use of electronic cameras and videotape recorders, and fewer and fewer film projectors are to be found. But what does this mean? Do we need a new approach to this new medium? Are the skills of the film producer outmoded? The answer is absolutely not! The motion picture, whether electrons on magnetic tape or crystals imbedded in celluloid, is the same. The differences for a cameraman or a lighting technician are minor adjustments. Each year video changes, and there is a good chance that the color film that still runs through a large number of Arriflexes and Mitchells will be gone by the year 2000. For the present, film and video are both viable, each with its own strengths and weaknesses, and a wise producer learns to deal with both.

Film has advantages: 1. It is a better medium for original production. Until the heralded high-definition television is perfected, it is impossible to match the quality of 35mm film with television technology. Although technically close to 16mm film, videotape has some qualities that cause people still to prefer the "look" of film. 2. Film is the only international standard for distribution; television is mired down in different standards, which suffer greatly when converted. 3. Film can be shown to large audiences easily. Television is moving in the right direction, but despite $18,000 projectors, the image suffers from the expansion to a large screen. 4. Film equipment is relatively simple and reliable, making it easier to use in remote locations or rough climates.

Film is the medium of choice for most directors, but the choice is no longer theirs because of the overriding economic benefits of videotape. Video is faster and cheaper than film on the whole while being very close in quality. It is easy to edit, which is particularly good for producers because they can sit in on edit sessions and watch the progress of the production. Special effects and titles can be inserted with the ease of operating a typewriter, and dupes can be made quickly and cheaply.

There are definitely aesthetic differences between film and video, but they grow fewer every year. Video has been able to show that in situations requiring extensive use of the equipment, such as television news, it can produce an image of adequate quality for much less money. That is the bottom line. Film still is indispensable in animation and the medium of choice for short programs. It is also vastly better than the American (NTSC) standard when shown on foreign television systems.

Many people are drawn to work in film because they have

been touched by movies in some way and become ensnarled in the mystique with which the press surrounds them. It can be a romantic career as a merchant of dreams. If you listen in on conversations between workers on a set, or between members of the press covering films, their fascination with their work shows through. Even those who crank out "B" films aimed at soft-tops in Georgia reserve a special respect for the potential of their trade. They enjoy their work. Underpaid and overlooked as they may be, when people have worked in film for a few years they rarely leave for a different line of work. It makes sense to work with something that is more than just a way to make a living. Americans pioneered the medium of film. In a sense we wrote the grammar of film, and we are as much in love with the silver screen today as we were when *Birth of a Nation* sent shivers up the nation's spine. Film has a history; it has a pantheon of stars who conjure up our cultural history.

Television, on the other hand, is in its infancy. Milton Berle, Sid Caesar, and Ernie Kovacs are founding fathers. Certainly there has been some originality, but much of what has constituted television to date is modified cinema. From the beginning, television was looked at primarily as a business. Film is, of course, a business also, but not in the same sense. Fewer people work in television because they love it; the salaries, yes, but the mystique? the feeling of getting a message across? the glamor? Few people apprentice themselves to great television figures. Television is still growing, however, and I expect that an increasing number of people will take the time to make serious programs. Those people will be mixed with the majority who are occupied cranking out filler. It is my personal observation that those with a concern for their message and medium have a full understanding of film's heritage and myriad forms of expression, while the others are merely students of the business of broadcasting. Many people who work in film can't make the transition to television: Without the mystique, it's just another job.

For the next few years film will continue to be used for the best productions of all kinds. In 1984 a study by Eastman Kodak showed that 80 percent of television programs originated in film. In that year 800 TV programs were shot on film, 45 percent on locations outside studios, and Kodak chalked up its best year for film sales in history. High-definition television cameras are likely to change this situation within the next ten years, but for the immediate future the growth of video is most interesting on a different level: the low end. Inexpensive and compact video cameras combined with VHS or Betamax video recorders are already revolutionizing recreational motion picture-taking as well as low-budget promotional and industrial productions. Unfortunately, the equipment is so automatic that anyone can operate it. This is a blessing for beginners, who are freed from concerns about f-stops and even focusing and can immediately concentrate on what they are shooting. But it gives people a feeling that a professional is not necessary, and it leads to a kind of sloppiness not found in people who have been trained in the use of film equipment. Film technology, which is less automated, forces one to understand the theory and practice of proper exposure and creative use of depth of field and to move the camera instead of pumping the motorized zoom.

Most programming recorded on videotape is shot with more than one camera in well-equipped studios with large crews that are usually unionized. You measure the cost of a production in minutes, and heaven forbid that anything goes wrong, because you will probably have to vacate the studio for the next program being shot there. Video producers are accustomed to making deadlines and working under pressure. Film producers tend to work with small crews and take their time. The kind of compromising done in a studio is anathema to a filmmaker.

Of course, when the show has been put on either tape or film, the business aspects are the same. That is one reason why few people are concerned over a future shift to television technology: Most of the industry is unaffected. They are dealing with "motion pictures," and that is the bottom line. Marshall McLuhan, in *Understanding Media*, pointed out some of the social and psychological differences between film and video. He spoke of film as a "hot" medium, for example, whereas video was "cool." We shall not wax philosophical regarding the two media. From the point of view of one entering the motion picture business, video has given the industry new growth and increased potential. The rhetoric hasn't changed, and neither have the rules of effective entertainment, enlightenment, and persuasion.

Chapter V

Commercials

"The only part of television which has fulfilled its promise at all is the commercial."

Paul Goodman

Commercials have become a part of our culture. In 1980, $25 billion was spent by all advertisers, as much as was spent on higher education. Presidential candidates chide each other with phrases like "Where's the beef?" and major companies spend millions for a few seconds of television air time to get their product in front of the people. It is not unusual for a company like Dr. Pepper to spend $250,000 for a thirty-second spot.

Some of the largest incomes in the film business are in the field of commercial production. Aside from the expensive prime-time ads, hundreds of affiliated stations and cable systems need commercials. If the commercial world appeals to you, making an inexpensive ad can be the best way to develop a demo reel.

Big-budget commercials are handled by advertising agencies. New York has over one hundred agencies, and each works with ten to fifteen producers and directors operating as independents. A company usually chooses an agency to do its advertising. Once the account is secure, the agency maps out a strategy, which usually includes magazines and radio as well as film. The films planned are then committed to a storyboard. The storyboard traditionally has been a series of pictures representing each scene on a commercial and each shot in that scene. These "boards" are now being done on tape. Basically, all this takes is the videotaping of the traditional storyboard, but the result is closer to the final commercial, and it helps the advertising agency explain its idea to the client. If there is still any doubt about the idea, a test commercial is made on 16mm film and

87

shown to selected audiences with a questionnaire; but once the idea is firm, the director takes over and shoots it on 35mm film. Regional ads are made on 16mm film, and video is used for the least expensive of the lot.

Directors can make a good income, although not always steady, from commercials; $70,000 is not out of line for a 30-second American Express commercial, and it is completed in less than a month. Getting to that position isn't easy, however. Convincing an agency means showing them a reel of your work, and that remains the key to getting started. I have known people who have used their own money to make a commercial for a fictitious product just to use in their reel. The competition is so stiff for commercials that an agency can often demand that you demonstrate skill in making a specific kind of film: testimonial, tabletop, medical, etc.

When the commercial finally goes into production, little has been left to chance. All of the client's and the agency's people show up on the set with the production crew, and working on

At the Brooklyn Model Works, Aleks Rosenberg, John Fraker, and John Kunch work on preparing a shot for a BMW commercial.

one of these shoots can explain the whole process at once. Commercials are designed to get people to buy things, want things, feel uneasy about the smell of their underarms—and that is the bottom line. In a way it seems a pity that some of the best talent in the film business is engaged in making them.

If you are interested in trying for a job with an ad agency, you will not often read about an opening in the New York *Times* classified pages. Work is obtained by hanging out in the right places, asking if you can do something. Meet people and try to get involved on the ground floor. In this business, as in show business, everything revolves around whom you know and word of mouth. Cynthia Freeland of ATI Video Enterprises in New York says, "I've never gotten a job cold—never. At certain points in my life I've sent out résumés and couldn't get arrested; the job opportunities I've encountered were usually through somebody I knew."

Remember that all agencies deal with newspaper campaigns, radio, television, and often trade shows. They employ a wide range of talents. In New York, 5,000 actors make their living primarily from commercials. The filming of a commercial is a very small part of an agency's work.

One last note on commercials. The development of computerized graphics for special effects (like those in *Tron*) is capturing everyone's imagination in the film and video business. The expense of the hardware has limited the experimentation to a few features and commercials. The machines, with names like ADO, DVE, and Mirage, can shatter, twist, colorize, and digitalize an image, then spin it off into infinity like a flying saucer. It isn't easy to make one of these $300,000 machines do this, however; it takes a knowledge of computer programming for many effects.

Like other electronic devices, the cost should come down, and when that happens the field of computer graphics should expand in many directions. Having an understanding of these devices could be invaluable.

To get a better idea of what it is like to make commercials, I talked with John Fraker, a young director who has done commercials for a long list of clients, including American Express and BMW, but who still considers himself a beginner.

RM: How did you get interested in making commercials?

JF: Perhaps I should go back a bit. I got interested in film through making a series of documentaries, but there was no money in them and before long I had to find some sort of work that would pay. I tried everything from silk screening T-shirts to typesetting and finally decided that I could make it as an editor. I went around New York with a guidebook put out by MPE listing the editing houses and blindly knocked on doors. After several weeks of this I finally stumbled onto a job editing commercials. I had the documentaries that I had edited to show and that helped, but I think it was my timing more than anything else that got me that start. I stuck with it and learned a lot, but a chance came up for a job with Channel 5 in New York at a salary twice what I was earning, so I grabbed it. I suppose in retrospect I learned from that job too, but what a grueling schedule I had. I can see why so many editors for TV news burn out or go a little off their heads. The pace is breathless and the quantity of work is amazing—and the next day you are right back in it again. I started to save some money from my overtime, and pretty soon I felt that I could strike out on my own. I formed a partnership with a friend, Aleks Rosenberg, and the two of us decided to make "Rock Videos."

RM: They must have been fun to make.

JF: Oh yes, we had a great time. The sets were often in exotic spots like the middle of Times Square. I'd always been a rock 'n' roll fan, so it was fun to be able to work with groups like Arrowsmith and Foghat.

RM: Did you manage to make a profit?

JF: Just barely. We started out doing them for cost, and in some cases less than cost, just to get started. But once we got started—or at least we thought we had—we were never able to pry enough money out of the record companies or the groups to make a reasonable profit. It seems that we were competing with other beginning groups, where we had been the year before, and they were just as willing as we had been to cut their margin of profit. It just looked as if we would never break out of that competitive spiral, and the two of us threw in the towel after a couple of years. Aleks went into animation and industrials, and I turned to commercials. Toward the end of our partnership, we had done a commercial for American Express, and the profit was great. It was over in a short time, and there were no hassles about money. They simply wanted a quality job and were willing to pay the price. They also left us alone, in contrast to the MTV spots we did. The record company representatives were not reliable. They would agree to do something crucial, like obtaining the actors, and then forget. We even got into some lawsuits with our clients over their negligence, but none of this kind of aggravation occurred on a commercial set. They paid and it was on to the next, organized and efficient.

RM: Has it been hard trying to locate clients?

JF: Hard is not the word for it. I have found it very hard to break into the circle of people who make these commercials. I am constantly on the phone trying to get a chance to show my reel. I rented a nice office in midtown and developed a logo and calling card. My phone bill is ridiculous. I keep calling people until they are tired of putting me off. I know that I have a good reel—I'm confident that if they see it they will eventually give me some business. I only hope I can hold on long enough for that to happen. I've gotten some small jobs, doing inserts for commercials, enough to keep me going, but if I begin to land some of the bigger jobs I will only have to do a few a year to make a reasonable income.

RM: Have you any advice for beginners in this field?

JF: There has been a lot of talk in the trades recently about what the agencies are looking for. *Backstage* had an article pointing out that the agencies were looking for young people with experience in an established production house. They need directors, but they aren't willing to take any chances. It is definitely a "coattail" situation. To get started you ned to apprentice yourself to an established director and hope his references will carry enough weight to get you under way.

RM: Then they aren't willing to take chances?

JF: Precisely, and a lot has to do with the budgets. Procter and Gamble 30-second spots are budgeted at $50,000 and up. With that kind of money nobody wants to take a chance, so a well-established director can demand an enormous fee because he knows he is a safe bet. Everybody in the agencies is afraid to take a chance, because if something goes wrong they'll be the one called on the carpet.

RM: Is there any sign that things will be changing?

JF: Not at all; in fact the beginner is facing the worst possible time to enter the business. The agencies are looking for what they call the "feature" look. You know the MacIntosh ad that was shown a few times when they introduced the computer? It has a *1984* theme with a woman running through an audience of zombie-like people. Well, despite the fact that it was shown only a few times, the entire industry was affected, and the trend is to even larger budgets and elaborate sets. A friend of mine just left for England to shoot a 30-second commercial budgeted at one million dollars. With that kind of money they can get whoever they want.

RM: Is it worth waiting to get a big-budget commercial rather than something like a low-budget local spot that could keep you active?

JF: No, I want to hold out as long as I can. Working with major companies on national spots is such a pleasure. They know what they want, and they aren't cheap; they don't try to get you to change things to save them money, and they pay promptly. Working with record companies was torture. They were constantly changing their mind and really unaware of the intricacies of film production.

RM: Any parting thoughts for beginning directors?

JF: My story is pretty much typical. I've found that people with determination and perseverance will prevail. Talent helps, of course, but I've seen plenty of people who have made it pretty much on contacts alone and being able to know talent when they see it.

Chapter VI

Film as Business and as Art

"The way I look at the movie business is that the commercial directors are mining one end of the tunnel and I'm mining the other."
Norman Mailer

We have discussed many ways to find an entry point in the film business, but it is worth repeating that a college degree, although not essential in getting a job, can be useful in keeping it. The media are not like the circus passing through town, enticing kids to join up and leave home. They are a part of the fabric of our culture. Our culture values higher education, and although you might get a head start without it, when you hit your forties you will regret the omission.

Be sure the school can teach you, be sure it is equipped to make both video and film, because the future of film and tape is in a fusion of the two. Consult the Appendix for a list of colleges to consider, but let me make some specific recommendations. The best video programs are at the big schools; Boston University, the University of Texas in Austin, Brooklyn College of the City University of New York, and New York University are among the best and offer advanced degrees. One of the best schools for television at the undergraduate level is Ithaca College in Ithaca, New York, where even a freshman can take production equipment out into the field. Even if production isn't where you want to go with film and video, knowing how every stage works is important.

Feature filmmakers point to the University of Southern California and UCLA for good training. New York University has a large program, and Temple University stresses documentary theory and production. It is a good idea to check out the school carefully. Cornell, for example, has a generally good reputation but next to nothing in film and television.

Wherever you go, be careful not to get carried away by equipment and production. Most students discover too late that effective productions are well written and convey something of universal value. In discovering what to say and how to say it, you need to know where film has been, how the great films were put together. Becoming conversant with film history, which is the history of video as well, will prevent you, at the very least, from reinventing the wheel.

When you are ready to make your move, to center your career around motion pictures, be firm about what you want to do. It is sometimes hard to change once you become known in a certain capacity. Read the trade magazines. For an independent documentarian, the *Independent Film and Video Monthly* provides fund-raising tips and production information. *Variety* provides financial data on features. *Backstage* and *Show Business* provide gossip and help one keep track of what is being produced and how it is doing at the box office. *American Cinematographer* carries detailed how-we-did-it stories for production-oriented people. *American Film* keeps a critical eye on the industry at large. Reading these magazines gives you a feeling for the nature of the business and the kind of people who work in it.

For many years schools and even employers relied upon a test for what profession might be best for you. The Strong Vocational Test, it asked a series of questions that dealt with attitudes and personality and compared your answers with those of people working in various fields: lawyers, doctors, teachers. Of course, there was no category for filmmaker. It gave you an idea whether your attitudes and personality traits were similar to those of others in the profession you were contemplating. This test may not be available today, but you can conduct your own test informally by doing work, even if unpaid, as a production assistant and making your own observations. Be sure to ask yourself, "Can I stand the pressure?" "Could my family life be affected by the demands of the work?" "Do I really want to spend the rest of my life doing this?" "Do I have the talent?" The final question is the most important: "Do I like the people that I would be associating with during my career?" The question that you should avoid is, "Will I make a lot of money?" Never go into any profession on that basis. If you like what you are doing and have talent, you will do as well as in any profession associated with the arts. Of course, investment banking is in another league, but I am going under the assumption that if you could even contemplate such a career, you would not be reading this book.

If you are interested in being considered an artist, it isn't necessary for me to remind you of the difficulties facing you. All the arts involve financial risk. But rest assured that film is acknowledged as a valid form for artistic expression in all but a few musty corners of the art establishment. Most museums have theaters, and film screenings accompanied by lectures are the most popular events that these theaters offer.

Despite the cost and sporadic federal funding, the United States produces the most imaginative noncommercial experimental "film art" in the world. In a way it is ironic, because this kind of film seems to have more of a following in Europe than in the States. Most European countries provide full subsistence for selected filmmakers through grants directly from the government. The theory is that such support frees the artists from commercial pressure so that they can concentrate on their work. An American filmmaker receives support for individual projects based on his talent and the strength of the proposal submitted. Even well-known filmmakers have been turned down by the National Endowments. The most recent incidence of this was the refusal to fund a project of James Ivory and Ismail Merchant because the Henry James novel they had chosen was not deemed appropriate for a screen adaptation by the panel of assembled scholar/experts. This team of filmmakers is one of the most talented in the U.S., and the films they produced, *The Europeans* and later *The Bostonians*, are classics of the cinema.

With or without federal grants the American film industry moves ahead. Despite the inconvenience and insecurity associated with the competitive marketplace, it produces good work. The strain on the individual can be great, however; a strong ego and confidence in your talent are prerequisites of the trade. An artist is selling a completed work or the talent to complete another work on his terms. Most people are offering their talents to help complete a work on someone else's terms. This distinction is important because we are taught in college to be independent and creative, and it is difficult for some people to put aside their egos when they go to work for others. A lot of

Cartoon by Bruce Holman.

beginners are hired to help their bosses look good and have to sublimate their own interests for a while.

One final note: No matter what niche you seek in film, and how much independence you can carve out for yourself, it will be necessary to collaborate. Film, more than any other art form, is a group effort. Individuals interlock their roles in a chain from camera to projector, creating a process. Every individual affects the end result, and the end result is hard to disassemble into elements. Everything sort of blends together.

To get an idea of what it is like to survive as an artist making films, the best thing to do is talk with someone who actually makes films that are acknowledged as fine art and who has survived on the basis of that work. Doris Chase is such a person. I went to her Chelsea Hotel apartment and talked with her.

RM: How did you get started as a filmmaker?

DC: First off I should point out that I was really not that young when I began making films. I was married with two children and living in Seattle when I started making sculptures. I developed a reputation in that community and began to get substantial contracts for public works. I was able to get support for some filming on one of my kinetic works that involved dancers and some geometric shapes on casters. Part of the agreement for the filming was that I would have the rights to all the outtakes or the film that they didn't want. I took that scrap film and, with the help of some friends who knew more about film than I did, made *Circles*. I showed this "abstract" film around Seattle, and it attracted some attention. It was 1969, and there wasn't a lot of experimental film around then. Shortly after the film had been shown, I ran into a man from Boeing who was in charge of their computers. He manipulated the imagery I had in *Circles* with those enormously powerful computers, creating a series of multiple images that excited me about the potential of film as an art form. Of course, there was little I could do with this experimental work in Seattle, so I mailed it off to a film festival in

New York, where it was reviewed in the New York *Times*, something that now seems incredible to me.

RM: Is that what brought you to New York?

DC: Yes, that and the realization that I simply needed to get away. New York and perhaps Los Angeles are the only places where you can make the contacts to enable you to survive. You have to go to where things are happening.

RM: Have things changed since then?

DC: It is even harder today. Then I was a bit of a novelty. Women in film were attracting attention, and the experimental film was undergoing a period of popularity. Unfortunately, that period has pretty much come to an end. Despite the fact that there is still plenty of originality around, the novelty has worn off.

RM: How have you survived over the past fifteen years?

DC: Pretty much on the combination of lecture fees and rentals of my films. I sell a few prints, but I don't really make that much. Recently I have been selling my films on videocassette, and it is a much better idea. I sell a short film on 1/2-inch cassette for $275. That is less than the print costs of a film the same length. I think the videocassette may be the best thing that has happened to our business in a long time. Librarians tell me that they expect to make a complete switchover to videocassette within the next ten years.

RM: What about the idea of selling your work directly on cassette?

DC: The people who are buying cassettes now want *Jaws* and entertainment, but I expect a time will come when they will want to pick up a cassette of the kind that I do. Some people are trying it out in Video Shacks in New York with cassettes going for $29.95 or so.

RM: So you are optimistic about the future?

DC: Yes I am, but the problems are the same. Distribution is still the major problem facing an artist. I spend 95 percent of my time writing letters and proposals and on the phone trying to line up a screening or lecture. I'm selling myself most of the time. I'm envious of Shirley Clarke, who lives a few floors above me, because she is so good at selling her work... I'm constantly reminded that you really have to hustle your work; your work doesn't sell you. I used to think that I could go to a town and give a lecture, do my shtick, and that would be enough. Today I go straight to the library and introduce myself to the person who buys the prints. More often than not it ends up in a print sale. I feel like a baker at times: All I want to do is bake bread, but somebody has got to sell what I bake if I expect to continue.

RM: Have you any words of wisdom for those who are interested in making films or video as fine art?

DC: First off, don't be depressed by my pessimism. Film is coming to the end of a cycle, but video is only beginning, and it will be several years before the reservoir of interest out there will evaporate. It has always been this way for artists in any medium. Very few ever make it to the point where they can support themselves well on their work alone. What any aspiring artist needs to know is how to make a living, along with knowing how to produce art works. By that I mean something that can earn a salary; waiting on table, stockbroker, cameraman on feature, etc.

RM: Did you ever feel a pressure to make films or tapes because you thought they would sell?

DC: Certainly, but I found that whenever I did something because I thought people would like it, I failed. I just couldn't operate that way. I have to work on what appeals to me and try to avoid compromise, which isn't hard. There isn't enough money in what I do to tempt me into compromising.

RM: Any last words on how to make it in noncommercial short films?

DC: Learn the basics in verbal and written communication. Learn to spell and write in clear simple prose. Be able to type and explain to people what you want to do; be able to get an idea across. A lot of young people in their haste overlook these basics.

Minorities in the Media

There has never been a better time for members of minority groups in the United States to get involved with film, television, and radio. This has not been the case until very recently. Shortly after the riots that tore through Detroit and other cities in the mid-1960's, the President formed a national committee to find out what could be done to stop such violence. The Kerner Commission, as the group of politicians and businessmen became known, produced a scathing report in 1968 that pointed the finger at the broadcast media. The report confirmed the suspicion that the American broadcast industry had not opened itself up to minority representation. Less than 5 percent of the industry were members of minority groups.

To help rectify this situation, the federal government provided funding for training programs at all levels in film, television, and radio. One of the first training programs literally rose from the ashes in Detroit and was aimed at educating young blacks with the hope that they would consider a career in television or film. I was the director of that project in 1971, and I came out of it feeling that we had begun to unlock a tremendous potential. The students seemed to have a natural affinity for the field. Specific statistics are hard to find, but I think it is fair to say that there has been a marked increase in the number of blacks in film and television, both in front of and behind the cameras. An organization, The Black Filmmaker Foundation (1 Centre Street, New York, N.Y. 10007), has recently begun to package films by black filmmakers, helping both the individual producers as well as the causes they address. Denise Oliver and Warrington Hudlin are two of the most active members of this group. Hudlin has produced several influential films (*Black at Yale*, *Street Corner Stories*), and Oliver has made several tours in Europe with films by American black independent filmmakers.

Other minority groups have not fared as well. Programs for native Americans were widely scattered, and very few native Americans are involved with film or television in any capacity. A notable exception is the Mohawk film production center on the St. Regis Reservation in northern New York and Ontario, Canada (the reservation actually spans the border near Cornwall,

Ontario). In the late 1960's the National Film Board of Canada sent a small crew with George Stoney to St. Regis to help the Mohawks state their grievances against the customs procedures at the border crossing that went through their land. The film that came out of that collaboration, *You Are on Indian Land*, remains one of the landmark films dealing with the problems of native Americans. The leader of the Mohawk crew on that film, Mike Mitchell, is now the director of the film and videotape production center on the St. Regis Reservation, which tries to build unity in a nation of native Americans that has been divided by religion, treaties, and hard times. The most recent film to come out of the center is *Iroquois Social Dance*, which features the Akwesasne Singers doing traditional dances of the Iroquois in a realistic and natural setting. Aside from the land disputes that erupted in the 1970's, which generated a few documentaries that were highly critical of government policies, the most prominent use of film has been in the preservation of traditional crafts and customs of Indian culture. People like Mike Mitchell are aware of the erosion of traditional values that has taken place over the past decade, as Indians have come into contact with the surrounding culture. Film and video help to slow that change and provide a record for future generations.

America has always been a melange of minorities. Hispanic filmmakers hold an annual film festival in New York, and there is now an Asian-American filmmakers' organization. Many beginning filmmakers have found that appealing to a specific group can help with initial support for productions. Brian DePalma's short film *Italianamerican* played to crowded theaters in New York—crowded with people with Italian roots wanting to see a film that they could identify with. Although they will not come out and say it, granting agencies like the National Endowments try to help minority groups get funding for films. Mirra Nair received enough grant money to produce *So Far from India*. She returned to her native New Delhi to capture the story of an Indian-American immigrant and his family. Groups made up of immigrants from India began to invite her to show the film and to discuss the problems it addresses. The reputation of the film grew, and she soon found herself screening to large and diverse groups on a variety of occasions.

Women in the Media

Starting in the mid-1970's a boom in productions by women began. All of a sudden women were the "in" subject, and granting agencies couldn't seem to find enough female producers to whom to give money. Hundreds of films on, by, and for women were turned out, catapulting a handful of women filmmakers to national prominence overnight. The illusion that film was somehow a male province was quickly dispelled.

One of the reasons that the reaction was so strong was because very few women were actually involved with production. Since the beginning, women were the majority in film librarian positions and prominent in marketing and granting agencies but found it difficult to break into the ranks in production. For one reason, film equipment was bulky and heavy and simply a great physical strain to haul in and out of cars and up and down stairs and then try to hold steady for any length of time. With the advent of the transistor and some innovations in camera design, the bulk began to disappear by the mid-1970's. Along with more compact cameras came quartz bulbs, which greatly reduced the burden of location lighting.

Today more and more women are becoming actively involved with production. Several have run successful production companies. Nell Cox, who built a reputation on her documentaries *Operator* and *French Lunch*, launched a career making dramas and has completed several, including a PBS Special, *Liza's Pioneer Diary*. Claudia Weill, who gained recognition by shooting with Shirley MacLaine in China, is co-owner of a small production company. Bri Murphy has produced several substantial productions in California under her company name, Sombrero Productions.

Chapter **VII**

Teaching Film

"Moviemaking is like sex, you start doing it, and then you get interested in getting better at it."

Norman Mailer

During the past twenty years a lot of talented people became attracted to the power of film, either to amplify their voice on the problems of America society or go get their particular dream out to people in large numbers. The writers of the 1940's and 1950's turned to the media in the 1960's because that was the way to reach people, that was the way to motivate. The Vietnam war was, as Marshall McLuhan put it, "a hot war on a cold medium." Vietnam was not only fought on the tube for Americans and the world, it was debated there also. The demonstrations were in large part media events, very much aware of the presence and power of being seen on television.

The way one brought things to television twenty, or even ten years ago was through film. Television was basically a system for transmitting and receiving images, not a medium that would record life outside a studio. Recording the images of that tumultuous period became the obsession of young people, and film as an academic discipline became inevitable. Out of these first classes sprang hundreds of aspiring filmmakers. Film festivals for short films were receiving over 400 entries in the early 1970's. People had discovered that film was not only effective, it was fun, and the frustrations of funding and the technology were minor inconveniences. A group called the Foundation for Independent Film and Video sprang out of this "film movement," and they have helped to focus on problems facing people in the media first by bringing them together socially, and then by lobbying and exerting political pressure.

But as the "movement" progressed, individuals found it difficult to get beyond the first or second film. Funding was hard to come by, and the result was a turn to teaching, even by people who were not naturally suited for the work.

Curiosity about this new power to record images and sound gave many the feeling that they were wresting power from the "establishment," and it was in that atmosphere that students turned in droves to film study in the early 1970's. Their teachers were often not much older than they. It was a new discipline; some said it was the only truly American art form and the first to emerge in the twentieth century. In any case, it grew rapidly and created a need for teachers.

Confusion still exists in the traditional ranks as to what kind of training a film teacher should have. At first few questions were asked, but starting in the 1980's colleges began to crack down: "If you are an artist go get a Master of Fine Arts if you want to teach here!" "If you are a critic, you should have a PhD like our English professors." Of course, college film teachers saw this coming, and graduate schools that train teachers began to add or amend programs to include film. Most of the training programs grew out of Speech Departments, and the addition of this new area of study prompted many to change their department name to Communications or Media Studies. Such changes have been so numerous that it is hard to know just what a "Communications" department does any more. The best way to tell is to check on the training of the faculty, which can be done by looking through the listings in college catalogs. Find out in what subjects they earned their degrees, and you will get an idea of how they will teach a class enigmatically called Media or Theory of Communication.

This discussion deals with film teaching at the college level. There is little opportunity to teach film at the high school or grade school level. A few large cities have special high schools, such as Edward R. Murrow in New York, that prepare students for careers in film or television. Most secondary schools, however, teach film only as part of an art program, or perhaps as part of an English program if interested and motivated teachers are available. It takes more than interest or motivation to teach film at the college level, however.

As I have mentioned, colleges have embraced film study, but they have applied the same rules to the training of film teachers as to other faculty. That means that a prospective film teacher must obtain a terminal degree. Just what is a terminal degree? That depends on the department in which film is being taught, or if it is a film department, what division of the college it is in. If film is being taught in a School of Art, an MFA is considered terminal. A Master of Fine Arts can take up to three years to complete, and there is a wide variance as to the amount of work needed to obtain the degree. The MFA can make a lot of sense for filmmakers, since it requires a minimum of liberal arts courses and puts stress on what you can create. If you want to work in a film and television department teaching production, this degree is all you need, and most programs for the MFA are a lot shorter than those for the PhD.

The PhD is the principal degree for all college teachers. Although the MFA is accepted by colleges, the PhD is almost always preferred. It is often referred to as the "union card." Where another degree may suffice under certain circumstances, the PhD is universally accepted, giving its holder the assurance that his training will never be questioned when it comes time to renew the contract.

The problem for students who wanted to fill the positions in film that were opening up in the 1960's and 1970's was that graduate programs in the film didn't exist. The first programs to develop were appendages to other graduate degrees such as performing arts or speech. By the early 1980's a full collection of graduate programs existed. It appears that the rush to film has slowed, and the number of students entering training in the field has leveled off. A lot of smaller colleges are only now catching up with the bigger schools and feel they should have at least a token course or two to be thought up-to-date.

All in all, film is as good a field as any for a teacher with a PhD in the foreseeable future, but it will probably mean teaching at a smaller school and in a department kept small by the expense of the hardware. Although the community colleges and state colleges, where the growth is now, are bent on having a program or department in film, they are rarely able to put the money into the necessary equipment. Film is probably the most expensive subject to teach on a per capita basis, and that means that the administration keeps a watchful eye on what is being done. Colleges have become very cost-conscious of late, and several have hired young professors and turned them over to the students with nothing more than a classroom to teach with. Most beginning teachers, having just emerged from graduate school, are eager to take any position to get started and assume they will be able to find the funds somewhere. That will not be easy. Federal money for educational media has all but disappeared.

This situation has brought about a new attitude among educators. Many administrators are beginning to look at the commercial potential of film and television. Established programs like that at Brooklyn College, when threatened by declining enrollment, have started renting out their facilities. This gives students a chance to work on "professional" projects, and the school gains support for its equipment while opening positions for teachers who may not have the PhD but can be justified on the basis of their professional experience. If this situation continues for very long, friction could develop, or a split in the field. Teachers with PhDs rarely have any professional experience. They take a rigorous set of exams in languages and write lengthy papers tracing intellectual developments but have very little to do with the commercial use of film. Since so much of the use of film is aimed at product advertising, this is an ironic twist. Professors end up teaching film as a fine art—a very small segment of the total use of the medium—and ignore the bulk of business that is done with film. That may be all well and good, but it is not very useful for a student who would like to work in the industry.

So much for the specific field of film teaching. What of the idea of teaching at all? Most people are aware of the problems in secondary education today: relatively low salaries and demanding work. There is a good chance of these conditions improving in the near future. The outlook is for strong demand for teachers and a small supply. That situation usually enables well-organized labor groups to begin to exercise their strength and improve conditions and salaries. Even if conditions improve, however, the constant contact with young people and the involvement with their problems is enough to make teaching an exhausting profession.

College teaching can be a rewarding and satisfying profession. The school year for most two- and four-year schools is between eight and nine months, leaving enough time to get seriously involved in making films. The salary can provide a basis of security in an erratic business. Because the demand for college teaching positions is great, the salaries have been kept down. If you take a teaching positin with a master's degree (MA or MS), you can expect at least $16,000 a year as a first position. Of course that will mean obtaining a terminal degree, in most cases a PhD.

All teaching positions come up for review by the dean after at the most seven years, at which time the teacher's work is reviewed. The principal criteria are good teaching evaluations, creative activity, and service to the school and the community. For the latter category, that you are expected to work on various school committees. Popularity with your colleagues is probably the single most important factor, despite the fact that the American Association of University Professors gives most of the responsibility for the review to the dean.

The review is important because once a teacher has passed it, he or she has a lifetime contract and cannot be fired unless moral impropriety or something equally scandalous is involved. For this reason a lot of perfectly good teachers with clean records do not receive tenure. Schools are very cautious because they fear a lack of flexibility. It was this very problem of tenure that made it difficult for film to establish a beachhead in higher education. So many tenured professors were entrenched in traditional disciplines that the schools' hands were tied: they couldn't shift these older professors, many of whom thought film to be "popular" art and not the province of a liberal arts program, to teach the new courses.

Teaching is the only profession, available to the average individual, with this kind of lifetime contract, and we may see the end of it in the next decade. Universities are not going to let themselves get "tenuritis" or be stuck with a faculty that has no motivation to change with the times. The fact of the matter is that a lifetime contract gives a faculty member protection from capricious administrators or other faculty members who do not agree with his approach to learning. It permits a scholar to concentrate on long-term research and the kind of detailed studies that cannot be done in the competitive pressure of the commercial world.

To be successful as a teacher in college, aside from the obvious traits that all of us associate with teachers, one has to look beyond the matter of lecturing to classes. Although the criteria that are written out in contracts stress the contact with students, it is the ability to do valuable research or creative work that eventually separates the outstanding professor from his colleagues. Whereas a high school teacher may view the summer as a welcome vacation, for a college teacher the time away from classes is expected to be spent in the "advancement of knowledge." It is "free time" only in the sense that the people are free to spend it any way they want, but don't think that college professors have a lot of time off. If they do take it, they do not survive for long in an increasingly competitive environment. A college teacher should be independent and self-directed. Teaching is something that many scholars and artists do as a means to an end: It is a way to get paid to write books or make films that are important but cannot find support from the commercial world.

The top salary for a professor can reach $40,000 to $50,000 per year in the large universities. When you consider the expense and time it takes for training, this is well below the top figures for lawyers and doctors, but there is no other profession that can give as much freedom and security. Freed from commercial pressures, a professor is in a good position to discuss the world as it might be. Spiro Agnew, the infamous Vice President under Richard Nixon, once dubbed such people "effete intellectual snobs," a phrase that has remained with us because it so accurately reflects the anti-intellectualism that runs deep in American culture. Despite the fact that the general public tends to trust professors, the man in the street doesn't believe they have much usefulness in our culture. While the economy is strong, teaching and studying film will not only survive, but grow. If the economy falters and people become more practical, the field of film scholarship is likely to be curtailed.

Appendix

Film Production Grants

National Endowment for the Arts
2401 E Street NW
Washington, DC 20506

Each year the NEA puts out a guide to programs that outlines the divisions of the Endowment. Most of its funds are given to other arts organizations, which in turn dispense funds in their districts. The NEA does provide direct support for filmmakers through the Media Arts Program.

National Endowment for the Humanities
Humanities Projects in Media, Room 420
1100 Pennsylvania Avenue NW
Washington, DC 20506

This agency has five divisions. The division of general programs funds film and video productions with a humanities theme. To understand the guidelines and what a "humanity" is, write for the annual publication *Humanities Projects in Media*.

Creative Artists Public Service Program (CAPS)
250 West 57th Street, Room 1424
New York, NY 10019

Grants ranging from $3,500 to $10,000 to individuals who are residents of New York State.

Independent Filmmaker Program
c/o American Film Institute
501 Doheny Road
Beverly Hills, CA 90210

Grants from $500 to $10,000 to individuals for any kind of film. Selections made once a year by a panel. Write for the guidelines before applying.

Short Film Showcase
Foundation for Independent Video and Film
625 Broadway
New York, NY 10012

It is worth a visit to the Showcase to look through the library that the Foundation has accumulated for help in funding. The Showcase is aimed at helping independent filmmakers create a wider audience for their 16mm films through grants that pay for blowups to 35mm, so that the films can play in commercial theaters.

Public Broadcasting Service
Program Data Coordinator
475 L'Enfant Plaza SW
Washington, DC 20024
    or
Corporation for Public Broadcasting
Television Activities
1111 16th Street NW
Washington, DC 20036

The best way to approach PBS and CPB, the major funding agencies for television programming, is to take a proposal to your local station. If they like your ideas, they may join with you in seeking support. This help is necessary because the national agencies want to be sure that films they fund will be aired. For a direct application, or for details of how to show them a completed film, write to them directly.

The Foundation Center
888 Seventh Avenue
New York, NY 10106

Corporate, community, and independent foundations help a wide range of film projects. To discover what is available, consult the comprehensive reference book published by the Foundation Center, or visit its library.

For feature filmwriters, it is essential to have an agent. For a list of agents, write to:

Writers Guild of America
Agency Department
8955 Beverly Boulevard
Los Angeles, CA 90048

Film-related Unions and Guilds

Screen Actors Guild (SAG)
1700 Broadway
New York, NY 10019
  or
7750 Sunset Boulevard
Hollywood, CA 90046

Actors Equity Association
165 West 46th Street
New York, NY 10023

American Federation of Musicians
641 Lexington Avenue
New York, NY 10022

International Alliance of Theatrical Stage
  Employees and Moving Picture Machine Operators (IATSE)
7715 Sunset Boulevard
Hollywood, CA 90046
  or
1515 Broadway
New York, NY 10036

National Association of Broadcast
  Employees and Technicians (NABET)
1800 North Argyle
Los Angeles, CA 90028
    or
1776 Broadway, Suite 1900
New York, NY 10019

Writers Guild of America
22 West 48th Street
New York, NY 10036
    or
8955 Beverly Boulevard
Los Angeles, CA 90048

American Society of Composers, Authors, and
  Publishers (ASCAP)
1 Lincoln Plaza
New York, NY 10023

Recommended Periodicals on Film

Cineaste
333 Sixth Avenue
New York, NY

> Covers political cinema in Africa, Latin America, Europe,
> and North America; quarterly.

Film Comment
Film Society of Lincoln Center
1865 Broadway
New York, NY 10023

> Serious criticism of features; six times a year.

Film Culture
1499 General Post Office
New York, NY 10001

> The most complete coverage of noncommercial films, with
> emphasis on the avant garde; quarterly.

Film Library Quarterly
Box 348, Radio City Station
New York, NY

Regular coverage of features, plus commentary on documentaries and occasional reviews of experimental films and video.

Film Quarterly
University of California Press
Berkeley, CA 94720

One of the older magazines; covers feature films, with an occasional review of short films.

Variety
154 West 46th Street
New York, NY 10036

Required reading for all producers, it tracks box-office results for the industry; weekly.

The Independent
Foundation for Independent Video and Film
625 Broadway
New York, NY 10012

The best magazine for people who make documentaries and short noncommercial films and video. Covers grant deadlines, film festivals, tips on production and distribution techniques; 10 times a year.

Sight and Sound
81 Dean Street
London WIV6AA, England

Reviews and occasional coverage of independent and avant-garde films; quarterly.

SMPTE Journal
863 Scarsdale Avenue
Scarsdale, NY 10583

Published by the Society of Motion Picture and Television Engineers. Carries technical articles on motion picture and television systems and equipment; monthly.

Video Pro
Vidpro Publishing Co.
350 East 81st Street
New York, NY 10028

Behind the scenes in EFP (electronic field production), with practical articles aimed at those who are entering the business; monthly.

Millimeter
826 Broadway
New York, NY 10003

Covers commercials, with emphasis on film and tape production; monthly.

On Location
6777 Hollywood Boulevard
Hollywood, CA 90028

Film and video production articles with wide appeal in the industrial, educational, and commercial markets; monthly.

Film Distributors That Handle Short Films

Carousel Films
1501 Broadway
Suite 1503
New York, NY 10036

Time-Life Films
Time and Life Building
New York, NY 10020

New Yorker Films
43 West 61st Street
New York, NY 10023

Picture Start
204 West John Street
Champaign, ILL 61820

Bernice Coe and Associates
65 East 96th Street
New York, NY 10028

Phoenix Films
470 Park Avenue South
New York, NY 10016

MacMillan Films, Inc.
34 MacQuestern Parkway South
Mt. Vernon, NY 10550

Film-Maker's Cooperative
175 Lexington Avenue
New York, NY 10016

Learning Corporation of America
711 Fifth Avenue
New York, NY 10022

Contemporary Films
267 West 25th Street
New York, NY 10001

The Museum of Modern Art
Department of Film
21 West 53rd Street
New York, NY 10019

Film Festivals and Awards

Academy Awards
8949 Wilshire Boulevard
Beverly Hills, CA 90211

> Documentaries, short subjects, etc.
> Deadline: December
> Fees: None
> Awards: Statuettes (Oscars)

American Film Festival
43 West 61st Street
New York, NY 10023

> Educational films
> Deadline: January 15
> Fees: $35–$100
> Awards: Ribbons

Ann Arbor Film Festival
P.O. Box 283
Ann Arbor, MI 48107

> Documentaries, shorts, with an art orientation
> Deadline: February
> Fees: $17
> Awards: $2,000–$3,000

ASIFA Film Awards
Room 1018
25 West 43rd Street
New York, NY 10036

> Animation only
> Deadline: January
> Fees: $5 to $40
> Awards: Public screening for a year

Athens International Film Festival
P.O. Box 388
Athens, OH 45701

Wide range of features and short films
Deadline: April
Fees: $5 to $60
Awards: $3,000 total

CINE Awards
1201 16th Street NW
Washington, DC 20036

Views short films with an eye toward entering them
  in foreign festivals
Deadline: February 1
Fees: $15–$50, depending on length and if entrant is an
amateur
Awards: CINE Eagle Certificate
Note: All CINE does is enter your film in foreign festivals,
and they charge you a fee to boot for each one.

Hemisfilm
International Fine Arts Center
1 Camino Santa Maria
San Antonio, TX 78284

Wide range of 16mm and 35mm films
Deadline: February
Fees: Variable
Awards: $2,000

Independent Film Makers Exposition
Brooklyn Arts and Culture Association
200 Eastern Parkway
Brooklyn, NY 11238

Short (under 60 minutes) films
Deadline: January (end of the first week)
Fees: $10
Awards: At least $3,500, distributed according to length.
  All films screened are paid.

Sinking Creek Film Celebration
Box 3253 Davy Crockett Station
Greenville, TN 37743

Documentaries and shorts
Deadline: May
Fees: $25
Awards: $3,000 and production grants

U.S. Industrial Film Festival
1008 Bellwood Avenue
Bellwood, IL 60104

Industrial and educational films
Deadline: March
Fees: $65
Awards: Certificates

USA Film Festival
3000 Carlisle Plaza
Dallas, TX 75204

Shorts, documentaries, and some features
Deadline: February
Fees: $10
Awards: Certificates

Film Schools

American Film Institute Center for Advanced Film Studies
2021 North Western Avenue
Los Angeles, CA 90027
Highly selective; puts students in contact with professionals
who guest-lecture.

San Francisco State University
Film and Creative Arts Department
1600 Holloway Avenue
San Francisco, CA 94132
BA and MA with a creative artistic bent.

University of California (UCLA)
Theatre Arts Department
405 Hilgard Avenue
Los Angeles, CA 90024
  BA, MA, MFA, and PhD in a superior but very competitive program.

University of Southern California (USC)
Division of Cinema
School of Performing Arts
University Park
Los Angeles, CA 90007
  BA, MA, MFA, and PhD; new facilities and a competitive, comprehensive program.

Northwestern University
Radio-Television-Film
School of Speech
Evanston, IL 60201
  BA, MA, MFA, and PhD; general liberal arts and theory strong.

Southern Illinois University
Department of Cinema and Photography
Carbondale, IL 62901
  BA, MA, MFA, and PhD; strong photography program and film as a business.

University of Iowa
Speech Department
Iowa City, IA 52242
  BA, MA, and PhD; emphasis on film theory and criticism.

Boston University
Department of Broadcasting and Film
School of Public Communications
640 Commonwealth Avenue
Boston, MA 02215
  BS and MS; strong broadcasting program.

Ithaca College
School of Communications
Ithaca, NY 14850
BS in film, photography, and television; probably the strongest program in the U.S. strictly for undergraduates.

New York University
Department of Cinema
51 West Fourth Street
New York, NY 10012

Syracuse University
College of Visual and Performing Arts
Syracuse, NY 13210
BS (TV-R Dept.), BFA, and MFA; excellent variety and depth, particularly in graduate programs.

Ohio State University
Department of Photography and Cinema
Columbus, OH 43210
BA, MA, and BFA; diverse program that stresses film theory and criticism.

Temple University
Department of Radio Television and Film
Philadelphia, PA 19122
BA, MFA; emphasis on documentaries.

University of Texas
Department of Radio-TV-Film
Austin, TX 78712
BS, MA, and PhD in communications; excellent facilities, including television studios.

California Institute of the Arts
24700 McBean Parkway
Valencia, CA 91355
BA and MA; an art school for those interested in animation and film graphics.

Showcases for Independent Film and Video Work

East Coast

Buffalo

Center for Media Study
S.U.N.Y. at Buffalo, 310 Wende Hall
Buffalo, NY 14214
   35mm, 16mm, Super-8, video; all genres.

Cambridge

Center Screen
University Film Study Center
Box 275 Cambridge, MA 02138
   16mm, video.

New York City

Anthology Film Archives
80 Wooster Street
New York, NY 10012
   35mm, 16mm, Super-8, video; avant-garde.

Artists Space
Fine Arts Building
105 Hudson Street
New York, NY 10013
   16mm, Super-8, Regular 8, video; visual arts-oriented.

Collective for Living Cinema
52 White Street
New York, NY 10013
   16mm, video; nonnarrative, avant-garde.

Global Village
Video Study Center
454 Broome Street
New York, NY 10013
   Video; documentary.

Kitchen Center for Video and Music
59 Wooster Street
New York, NY 10012
   Video; fine arts-oriented.

Millennium Film Workshop
66 East 4th Street
New York, NY 10003
   16mm, Super-8, Regular 8; avant-garde, experimental, personal.

Museum of Modern Art
11 West 53rd Street
New York, NY 10019
   35mm, 16mm, video.

New American Filmmakers Series
Whitney Museum of American Art
945 Madison Avenue
New York, NY 10021
   16mm, video; all genres.

New York Public Library
Donnell Film Library
20 West 53rd Street
New York, NY 10019
   16mm: documentary, children's, avant-garde; video: art, documentary.

Philadelphia

Walnut Street Theatre Film Center
825 Walnut Street
Philadelphia, PA 19107
   35mm, 16mm, Super-8, video; all genres.

Pittsburgh

Carnegie Institute
Film Section, Museum of Art
4400 Forbes Avenue
Pittsburgh, PA 15213
16mm, Super-8, video; avant-garde, experimental.

Pittsburgh Film-Makers Inc.
P.O. Box 7200
Pittsburgh, PA 15213
   16mm, Super-8; experimental, documentary.

Rochester

White Ox Films, Inc.
3690 East Avenue
Rochester, NY 14618
   16mm; animation, documentary, experimental, narrative.

Washington

The American Film Institute Theater
John F. Kennedy Center for the Performing Arts
Washington, DC 20566
   35mm, 16mm; documentary.

Midwest

Boulder

Rocky Mountain Film Center
University of Colorado, Hunter 102
Boulder, CO 80309
   16mm; avant-garde, experimental.

Chicago

The Art Institute of Chicago Film Center
Columbus Drive & Jackson Boulevard
Chicago, IL 60603
   35mm, 16mm; all genres.

Detroit

Detroit Film Theatre
The Detroit Institute of Arts
5200 Woodward Avenue
Detroit, MI 48202
   35mm, 16mm; animation, avant-garde, documentary, personal.

Lincoln

Sheldon Film Theater
University of Nebraska
Lincoln, NB 68588
    35mm, 16mm; all genres.

Minneapolis

Walker Art Center
Vineland Place
Minneapolis, MN 55403
    35mm, 16mm, Super-8, video; documentary, avant-garde,
    animation.

South

Columbia

Independent Filmmakers Film Lecture Bureau
South Carolina Arts Commission
829 Richland Street
Columbia, SC 29201
    16mm; all genres.

Houston

Rice Media Center
Box 1892
Houston, TX 77001
    16mm, Super-8; all genres.

Nashville

Tennessee Performing Arts Foundation
4304 Harding Road
Nashville, TN 37205
    16mm; all genres.

Rock Hill

Independent American Film Makers: Southern Circuit
c/o Winthrop College
Joynes Center for Continuing Education
Rock Hill, SC 29733
  16mm, Super-8, video; animation, documentary, experimental, personal.

West Coast

Berkeley

Pacific Film Archive
University Art Museum
2625 Durant Avenue
Berkeley, CA 94720
  35mm, 16mm, Super-8; all genres.

Los Angeles

Los Angeles Independent Film Oasis
2413 Rinconia Drive
Los Angeles, CA 90068
  35mm, 16mm; all genres.

Theatre Vanguard
9014 Melrose Avenue
Los Angeles, CA 90069
  16mm, Super-8, Regular 8; documentary, experimental, personal, student.

Pasadena

Pasadena Film Forum
P.O. Box 5631
Pasadena, CA 91107
  16mm, Super-8, Regular 8; avant-garde, documentary, personal, political, anthropology.

Portland

Northwest Film Study Center
Portland Art Museum
1219 Southwest Park & Madison
Portland, OR 97205
    16mm, Super-8, Regular 8, video; all genres.

San Francisco

The Cinematheque
c/o 339 Head Street
San Francisco, CA 94132
    16mm, Super-8, Regular 8; avant-garde, personal.

Eye Music; Filmworks Series Inc.
633 San Bruno
San Francisco, CA 94107
    16mm, Super-8, Regular 8; avant-garde, nonnarrative.

San Francisco Museum of Modern Art
Van Ness & McAllister
San Francisco, CA 94102
    35mm, 16mm; all genres of social/artistic merit.

San Francisco State University Cinematheque
1600 Holloway Avenue
San Francisco, CA 94132
    16mm; all genres.

Seattle

And/Or
1525 10th Avenue
Seattle, WA 98122
    Video; visual arts-oriented.

Media Shop Inc.
1505 10th Avenue
Seattle, WA 98122

Bibliography

American Film Institute. *Guide to College Courses in Film and Television*. Washington: Acropolis Books Ltd.

Barnouw, Erik. *Documentary: A History of the Non-Fiction Film*. London: Oxford University Press, 1974.

Bawden, Liz-Anne, ed. *The Oxford Companion to Film*. London: Oxford University Press, 1976.

Dick, Bernard F. *Anatomy of Film*. New York: St. Martin's Press, 1977.

Field, Syd. *Screenplay: The Foundations of Screenwriting*. New York: Dell Publishing, 1979.

Geduld, Harry M., ed. *Film Makers on Film Making*. Bloomington: Indiana University Press, 1967.

Higham, Charles, ed. *Hollywood Cameramen*. Bloomington: Indiana University Press, 1970.

Jacobs, Lewis, ed. *The Movies as Medium*. New York: Farrar, Straus & Giroux, 1970.

——. *The Rise of the American Film*. New York: Teachers College Press, 1968.

Katz, John Stuart. *Perspectives on the Study of Film*. New York: Little, Brown & Co., 1971.

Kopelman, Arie, and Crawford, Tad. *Selling Your Photography*. New York: St. Martin's Press, 1980.

Maltin, Leonard, ed. *The Whole Film Sourcebook*. New American Library, 1983.

————. *Behind the Camera: The Cinematographer's Art.* New American Library, 1971.

Margolin, Judith. *About Foundations: How to Find the Facts You Need to Get a Grant.* New York: The Foundation Center, 1975.

Mast, Gerald. *Film, Cinema, Movie.* New York: Harper and Row, 1977.

MacCann, Richard Dyer, and Perry, Edward. *The New Film Index.* New York: Dutton & Co., 1975.

McLuhan, Marshall. *Understanding Media.* New York: Signet Books, 1964.

Squire, Jason. *The Movie Business Book.* Englewood Cliffs, N.J.: Prentice-Hall, 1983.

Trojan, Judith, and Covert, Nadine. *16mm Distribution.* Educational Film Library Association, 1977.

White, Virginia. *Grants for the Arts.* Plenum Press, 1980.